Happy Birthday,

Mum

1994.

from

Ralph.

The Rebel Tyke

By the same author

Domes of Delight: a history of the Bradford Alhambra

Statue of J. B. Priestley with Bradford City Hall.
(Photograph by Tim Smith)

THE REBEL TYKE

Bradford and J. B. Priestley

By

Peter Holdsworth

Bradford Libraries

First published in 1994 by
Bradford Libraries
Central Library
Prince's Way
BRADFORD
West Yorkshire
BD1 1NN
England

ISBN 0–907734–36–7

Cover photograph: J.P. Barraclough's portrait of J.B. Priestlley
(Courtesy of Bradford Art Galleries and Museums)
Cover design by Kate Mellalieu-Heycock

Typeset and printed at Alden Press Limited,
Oxford and Northhampton, Great Britain.

Dedication

With loving thoughts, this book is in memory of the late Winnie Scott (or Winnie Priestley as was, as they used to say in J.B.P.'s Bradford). With esteem and all good wishes, it is also for Jacquetta Priestley (who loved her husband so much) and Tom Priestley (a son of whom any father would be proud).

The book is dedicated too to all other members of the remarkable Priestley family.

CONTENTS

Acknowledgements

My thanks to Reed Book Services and Rainbird Publishing for allowing me to quote from works by J. B. Priestley, and to the *Bradford Telegraph & Argus* for permitting access to its archives. Thanks also to Leslie Sands and Roger Suddards; to Liz Ambler, formerly of BBC Radio Leeds; Audrey Sykes for her kindness in giving me the photograph of Mabel Sealby; Ken Morrison for his anecdote about Roberts' pie shop; art critic John Hewitt for information about the Henry Moore exhibition; Jean Oldfield and Nell Walker of the Bradford Playhouse; Judith Hill and Belle Vue Boys' School; to Caroline Krzesinska (Bradford Art Gallery), Tim Smith (Bradford Industrial Museum), Elvira Willmott (Bradford Libraries), John Brooker (University of Bradford), and Stephen Homer (*Telegraph & Argus*) for photographs; Kate Mellalieu-Heycock for the cover design; and to Bob Duckett and colleagues of Bradford's Arts, Museums and Libraries service for help with the editing and publishing of *The Rebel Tyke*.

List of Illustrations

LIST OF ILLUSTRATIONS

Foreword

THE REBEL TYKE

What an inspired title for this excellent book about J. B. Priestley! He certainly was a rebel – almost every page throws up an example of his insurgent character.

But the fascinating quality is that he was, and always remained, a tyke. So what is a tyke? A Yorkshireman? Yes certainly, but can you have a Cornish tyke? I doubt it. A dictionary will give you definitions of a dog on the one hand and a surly ill-mannered fellow on the other. My tyke is neither of these but a glorious independent fighter of causes.

That J.B. was a tyke radiates through these delightful pages. Time and again he looks back to Yorkshire and to Bradford in particular. J.B. seemed all his life to think of his native city with love, affection, annoyance and criticism. Peter Holdsworth has captured the balance of these conflicting emotions splendidly.

To write a biography of someone you know well and within a generation of his death is no easy task. That other great tyke, Sir Titus Salt, was the subject of a sycophantic obsequious biography by his religious adviser, Balgarnie. As a result we know very little about the true character of Salt: we merely have a cardboard cut-out.

Not so with Peter's biography of J.B. He presents a warts-and-all portrait of the man. I had the benefit of knowing J.B. only when he was a rather old crusty chap. That in itself was a joy. But Peter knew him so well that this book reveals much of the broader character: strengths and weaknesses.

Peter sets J.B. in his rightful scene with fascinating attention to detail. To a reader anywhere this will be a crisp picture of Edwardian England and of post war (two of them) Britain. To a Bradfordian there are brilliantly written descriptions: the little brass figure of Punch inside Briggs' tobacconist, Mrs. Roberts' famous steaming pie and the Civic. To a Priestley enthusiast there is much to plunder here: the causes for the rebellions, the warmth of the Tyke.

Roots are vital to us all. Home is where the heart is. After reading Peter's book you are left with the unmistakable view that the rebel tyke never quite left home which, he wrote "always seemed to have the kind of ugliness that could not only be tolerated, but often enjoyed; it was grim but not mean."

FOREWORD

Peter Holdsworth had done a great service. He has written a wonderfully enjoyable book, yet at the same time it is a balanced record of Priestley's life. It achieves something some of the other biographers of J.B. do not. A great read.

Roger W. Suddards

Bradford, 1994

CHAPTER 1: PIGGY IN THE MIDDLE

Just before he retired in 1982 as deputy editor of Bradford's daily evening newspaper, the *Telegraph & Argus*, Kenneth Oddy, a journalist of integrity and distinction, handed me a photo-copy of a letter he had kept for 16 years.

"I want you to have this", he said. "I know how much you think of J. B. Priestley. I have a hunch you'll make use of it one day".

That day has come.

The letter, dated November 6th, 1966, had been written from his lovely home in Warwickshire by Bradford-born Priestley to Ken to thank him for an editorial he had published extolling the talents of J.B. The editorial was a rarity because from June 1953, when Priestley was named in a divorce case, until September 1973, when the author received the Freedom of Bradford, the relationship between Priestley and the chiefs of his hometown paper was frequently cool and occasionally abrasive.

The attitude of many Bradfordians during that period was harsher. It was often belligerently hostile.

All this antagonism caused a long if passing "family" squabble – a "family" one because Priestley, for all his leaving Bradford in the early 1920s, was never to see cut completely the umbilical cord between himself and the city. Throughout his life, Bradford never failed to influence and affect him, even though he was not a regional writer. He was very much an international one. But this didn't make the hostility milder. Domestic bickering has a habit of becoming acrimonious.

In the 1966 letter, Priestley, after expressing his gratitude to Ken Oddy wrote:

> The remainder of this letter is strictly private and must not be quoted. But it may supply you with material for another piece on a suitable occasion. I am told the cry has gone up 'What's he done for Bradford?'
>
> Now I am not a financial man or industrialist and so have never been able to pile up capital gains.
>
> I have earned a good deal of money, but, after taking care of various heavy responsibilities, it has gone in income tax and surtax. I cannot be expected therefore to behave like a rich man. But I have in fact done a good deal for Bradford.
>
> During the last forty years I have paid it more visits than I have to all other provincial cities put together. I have accepted innumerable invitations to perform public duties there, often at considerable inconvenience

1

and expense. For years I was a fairly active and interested president of the Bradford Civic Playhouse. I have declared over and over again what I owe to the city when growing up there before the First World War. In novels, plays, essays, broadcasts, I have paid tribute to the West Riding life and character. If there are better accounts of what it was like to be a youngster in pre-1914 Bradford than there are in 'Bright Day' and 'Margin Released', I would dearly like to read them.

I cannot live in or near Bradford because my wife and I are always having to go to London and so need to be nearer. For over forty years I have done all I possibly can, within reasonable limitations, for Bradford. And what, during those years, has Bradford done for me? A few lunches perhaps, a dinner or two. But I have had bigger and better lunches and dinners given me in London, New York, Moscow, Vienna, Prague, Copenhagen, Stockholm, The Hague, Delhi, Tokio and as far afield as Lima and Santiago, Chile.

On the face of it, Priestley's letter would seem to bolster the criticisms many Bradfordians had directed at him – Ingratitude for the good things life had brought him, touchiness, self-esteem, a moaner's inclination to spar, and a crabby tendency to undervalue any kindness Bradford had shown him.

But you could have won hands down a bet that nearly all those antagonists were not acquainted with him outside a few of his writings and broadcasts.

I was. In a long career as a Bradford journalist and theatre critic I met and corresponded with John Boynton Priestley many times, and I came to know (and believe understand) him well.

As soon as Ken Oddy gave me the copy of that letter, I sensed what was really behind Priestley's flash of indignation. It was hurt – the pain of a Bradfordian who, because of his forthright manner and unhypocritical character (and I have never come across a more honest man), had been slapped in the face too many times by a city he never ceased to cherish and which, through his works, he had made known to the world, no matter that he sometimes felt a solitary stranger there during his later years.

Many times have his words been quoted that: "The core of me is still in Market Street hearing the Town Hall chimes" and that "The West Riding working-class was in my blood and bones".

Yet seldom recorded have been these words: "If I do not live in the North, and have not done so for many years, I think I am still happiest up there". And these, when he was 86: "In Bradford they think and feel the way I do".

Sadly, too often and for too long, many Bradford people didn't think and feel the way Priestley did.

Nevertheless, ironically, many of Priestley's characteristics remained Bradfordian through and through. He never paraded his emotions. He recoiled from face-to-face compliments, let alone flattery. He could spot in a twinkling the sham in a person. If circumstances called for it, he was not afraid to call a spade a bloody shovel. He had no time for artificiality. He could be quick tempered, stubborn and curt. And like so many Bradford folk he could use an ostensible insult as a comic endearment – a form of affection many southerners find hard to understand.

Priestley, a master of dry wit, leg-pulling, irony and understatement, was not impressed by third-rate "star" personalities others cheered. He had a deep, inner sensitivity but relished the broadly comical. He enjoyed sending-up the pretentious. He responded to a challenge as eagerly as a street-fighter. And he was proud of his resonant Yorkshire voice with which he would speak slowly and deliberately with every booming word considered. "I always keep my vowels open", he jested.

Priestley's view of himself may surprise many. He said that the popular picture of him was of an "almost ferocious aggressiveness" whereas in fact he was "a friendly sort of chap; amiable, indulgent, affectionate, shy and rather timid at heart".

J.B.'s self-appraisal focused on only part of his character, of course. But what he said was correct. It is important to establish this because light must be thrown on some of the complexities of Priestley's make up (and he *was* extremely complex) if we are to explain what was behind those Bradford-Priestley estrangements of which there were too many before the final long-overdue reconciliation.

Those (and they were not few) who stood apprehensive of Priestley, fearing him as though he were a cantankerous Merlin, were surprised how affable he could be when they met him – although he wished they wouldn't try to touch him. "Funny how people want to touch you when you find fame," he said.

As for being indulgent, he was by nature compassionate and was tolerant in the encouragement he gave others, especially a young writer if he considered he or she had talent. If he thought otherwise, he said nothing (a lesson which could benefit the more destructive reviewers). When speaking of young writers collectively, he could be less forbearing.

Shy timidity is a deep-down characteristic of many northerners who have been subjected to the better-than-thou attitudes of London and the

Home Counties. A lot hide the shyness and timidity behind bluster and the bombast of inverted snobbery. Priestley, aware of this and adopting a carapace of confidence ("Cocky young devil!" some exclaimed during his early years) taught himself from youth how to make others believe he was as good as the next man and better than most. It didn't take him too long either to be able to move with apparent confidence in any kind of company, high, mighty or much less so.

The J. B. Priestley I got to know was kind, courteous, considerate, generous, roguishly funny, caring, romantic (although he would never have admitted that) and very lovable. And I quickly realised that in his own fashion, and while having little time for organised religion, he was extremely religious. There were a few who labelled him a mystic. In public, he revealed no sign of this. "But", as his son Tom told me, "I do believe he was more concerned with that aspect of existence than outsiders might believe, choosing instead to accept the stereotype of the 'bluff Yorkshireman' (what a horrid phrase). He clearly enjoyed a vigorous inner life – what decent writer doesn't?"

Numerous people tagged Priestley a man of common sense. They were way off mark. He was just the opposite. He was a man of immense UNCOMMON sense. Intuitively he sensed, nay seemed to be in contact with a power bigger than ourselves, and he constantly urged our responsibility to others. Just as constantly he sought all that was life-enhancing (a term he was to use again and again in his works). His socialism, even following the Labour Party's landslide victory after the 1939-45 war (and how glad he must have been to see the Tories thrashed) was never spelled with a capital S, because in reality it was benevolent, yet radical, liberalism. He never joined a political party. He detested bullies of every sort, from the bully State to the bully upper classes, from the bully bosses and the bully Trade Unions to the bully teachers, from bully pontificators to military bullies.

He rebelled against conformity for conformity's sake and against tyranny in any form, whether that tyranny came from church and chapel pulpits or was to be found on factory floor, in the boardroom, or at Westminster. He emphasised that it was the duty of a writer to rebel. This was advice from the horse's mouth. For John Boynton Priestley was THE rebel Tyke. How sad then to hear him say to a large luncheon gathering in his later life: "I think I like Yorkshire rather more than Yorkshire likes me".

Priestley was aware of two handicaps – his body and his face. Weighing fourteen stones or more for much of his life, he could seem to stand planted as formidably as an old-time football full-back (a position he played as a youth), as though he were defying anyone to challenge his might. At such moments he looked as hard and solid as a rock, as if there was no getting past him.

And his face? As broadly peasant-like as that of Dvorak whose chamber music and seventh symphony delighted him, its heavy cheeks, jowl and sacks beneath the eyes could make him look fierce at a time when he was brimming with cordiality. He called it "The treachery of my own face".

Two other features, however, did reflect Priestley's character faithfully. He had an impish, markedly upturned grin that would have suited a prankster leprechaun. And his eyes, at one moment shining, the next sombre and penetratingly astute, had the alertness of enduring youth. David Hockney was quick to spot this, and in his superb portrait of the author the eyes tell all.

Was J. B. Priestley moody? Yes. But when the moodiness was not induced by his wrestling with the inanities of mankind, it was more often caused by impatience or the rush of ideas which buzzed in his head like a million bees from boyhood onward. They were the devil to pin down and sort out.

Ideas, ideas, ideas. Hardly a writer in history can have been invaded by so many; and he confessed that too often they made him irritable with other people as he attempted to transform them into literary or dramatic shapes.

Because of those teeming ideas, Priestley's creative output was not simply colossal. It was as variegated as a mosaic . . . Nearly 40 plays, more than 30 novels, essay after essay, pamphlets galore, screenwritings for performers as diverse as Ronald Colman and Gracie Fields, autobiographical contemplations which were lessons in self-analysis, and his monumental *Literature and Western Man*, a study of novelists and poets over the centuries. (It took a year and a half to write and "half killed me".) It made the intellectuals who looked down on J.B., maintaining he was not fit to be in their company, look silly.

And there was more.

Priestley, who could be a compelling public speaker and who hated polarisation in politics, was not afraid to end his active sympathies if he became disenchanted or disillusioned – with, for example, the Labour Party with its State controls, top-heavy bureaucracy and adherence to trades union rules; and with the Campaign for Nuclear Disarmament whose founding he inspired and which he eventually saw being taken over by power-hungry propagandists.

His Sunday night *Postscript* talks on radio during the early part of the 1939-45 war were national events, giving hope to millions of a better world to come and anticipating (unlike the country's leaders) a great sea-change in social structures and conditions once victory had been won. The broadcasts became so popular that Priestley vied with Winston Churchill as the most inspiring personification of Britain's fighting spirit.

That Churchill didn't welcome the rivalry, and very likely was jealous of Priestley, is certain. But whether he had a hand in the sudden ending of the *Postscripts* is arguable. Some said he had. Others said he hadn't. What is definite is that J.B. himself emphasised in a Glasgow interview in October, 1940: "There is no question of my being 'bumped off for plain speaking'. When I said I had stopped of my own accord, and that my relations with the BBC were excellent, I was speaking the exact truth. I have simply stopped my talks because I think it is a good thing. The people get tired of hearing one voice. But if they have not tired and would like to get me back, well I am waiting in the wings."

So instead of the microphones, it was back to his typewriter which he worked with two fingers "pecking" at the keys like hungry hawks. Priestley broadcasts, apart from the *Postscripts*, went on apace. He continued throughout the 1939-45 war to broadcast regularly on the BBC Overseas Service, and was active in trying to get the Americans to enter the war.

Good writing is always a hard slog (odd that many people who rarely put pen to paper think it is a doddle) and Priestley knew it only too well. The difference between an amateur writer and a professional, he pointed out, was that an amateur wrote when he or she fancied it. A professional pitched in on a cold, wet Monday morning when he or she didn't fancy it at all.

It didn't take J.B. long either to note other drawbacks to being a full-time writer. *The Good Companions*, which made him a household name, was a mere two years old when, in March 1931, in an issue of *Nash's Magazine*, he confessed: "An author does not fall in love, get married, travel, or meet his friends. It is the other deep fellow who sits in the dark just behind, watching all the time, who watches himself falling in love, etc.".

He continued: "Many people, who do not know me, imagine that I am happy. But for the last ten years I have been engaged in this absurd task of earning a living by setting down words, and it has played the devil with me."

There was, however, another aspect to Priestley's character which too often has been mentioned as an aside. But it is vital if we are to understand him.

J.B. was never less than a realist (and often a marvellous humorist) when confronting the concrete matters of our existence. Yet, in being convinced that there was much beyond or outside our mundane experiences (and he loved to guess what that much might be), his mind and spirit were always open in wonder to the mysteries and magic of life – whether the mysteries and magic were to be sensed in his beloved and much visited Yorkshire Dales or in (and he adored it almost as much) the Arizona desert; or whether he experienced their enchantment in his multitude of dreams (real ones not daydreams) which seemed to take him out of or beyond wide-awake "realities" and Time dimensions.

Priestley was never so arrogant as to court the atheistic. We simply did not know the answers to the mysteries, he said – mysteries like Time and Space and whether or not immortality and eternity were possible. If immortality did exist, it was beyond his comprehension, he confessed.

In *Outcries and Asides* he wrote: "The weakness and hollowness of a time when science is dominant can be easily understood. At such a time we think we know everything when in fact we know nothing. I refer here, of course, to questions of real importance. Who are we? What are we doing here? What will happen to us? What is REALLY happening to us here and now? It is true that men in previous ages had no short and clear answers to such questions, but at least they did not pretend they knew everything but felt they were living in a mystery. True, the very idea of a mystery is a challenge to the scientist, and this is as it should be: we must not blame him. On the other hand, he must not behave as if he were a high priest of some dogmatic and bigoted new religion. He must not lose his temper, his manners, his sense of proportion, if some of us, making no great claim for ourselves, feel that now and again the veils of Time and Space have been briefly lifted. Sometimes he might tell himself, if only late at night, after a long day, that really we know nothing".

In *Over The Long High Wall* Priestley asked: "What happens at or after death? I don't know. Neither do you. However, I feel I can be allowed to do some guessing. I shall certainly have to risk the derision of 'the tough-minded' and the reproaches of 'the tender-minded', but then as a reasonable man I think the former are too pessimistic and the latter too optimistic. I refuse to believe that we come to an end as if we were so many steers in a slaughter-house. But also I cannot believe that after having sought and found mercy our immortal souls are granted illimitable felicity . . . We don't live for ever nor are we snuffled out when we have had our portion of passing-time. This seems to me a reasonable attitude to adopt, well away from the extremists and fanatical believers, from the fervent atheists, doing their familiar defiant-stoic act, and the theologians or evangelists still pretending to know about salvation and damnation."

Such Priestley speculations simply did not wash with the "intellectuals" who derided him, claiming his "philosophising" was too nebulous. At the same time many "ordinary folk" made mock of him for being "too intellectual", what with his references to Dunne, Ouspensky and Jung; to precognition, recurrence, intervention and consciousness; and to Time cycles, spirals and circles spinning out into another, perhaps parallel existence.

In other words, J. B. Priestley could not win. He was piggy in the middle as they say in Yorkshire.

He was accused of being woolly-minded. But if he was, so be it. At least he was not shoddy-minded he asserted during one Bradford visit. Again he couldn't win. There was an instant outcry from a West Riding (now West Yorkshire) manufacturer of shoddy (fibre made from old cloth, etc.) demanding how dare he denigrate the material which provided a livelihood for so many local workers. "We're not taking that from thee, Jack Priestley" was the message. It was a pointer to Bradford tiffs to come.

Priestley was often in hot water with those who accused him of too often being self-contradictory. How could he, for instance, confess at one moment to being a pessimist and the next moment describe one of his out-of-the-blue experiences when his whole being, for no apparent reason, was flooded with joy – while standing by his desk, when looking out of a window, when climbing the stairs, for example?

The explanation is that J. B. Priestley, who once teasingly called himself a life-enhancing pessimist, was a two-levels man. The outer level, some-times sombre and frequently ruffled, took rational account of the foolishness and stupidities of human beings and their dogmatic doctrines. The inner level, luminous with hope and charity, instinctively sought communion with wonders beyond definite clarification. Somehow, and often with laughter or chuckling irony, he harmonised the two. It was a feat of magic of his own making. And it was exhilarating.

At the time of his death at the age of 89 on August 14th, 1984 (it was within one month of his 90th birthday) his widow reflected: "I believe that one of the essential things about Jack was that he was so completely a whole, a man at one with himself. His mind and spirit were absolutely infused in his body, in his physical existence. That was the beginning of the source of his power."

Soon afterwards in a letter I received from Jacquetta Priestley she wrote of "the man I was so very fortunate to have married and loved for so long."

For years J.B. kept within hand's reach an observation by the poet Wordsworth. It read: "We live by admiration, hope and love".

"I quote it over and over again", he said, urging: "We have to go out and admire what we can admire. And once we can admire something let us give our hearts to it. We have to hope because despair is useless; and above all we have to love. Love is very strong, very enduring, and can last very many, many years. So if anybody wants a short guide to a decent life, let me offer this: We live by admiration, hope and love".

Priestley's pessimism (and he was never the Jolly Jack some branded him as though he were a clown in a literary circus) was a feeling far removed from the heart centre of his hope and affection. Yet that pessimism could rage. Convinced that things could get darker before they became sunny, he wrote in 1972 this devastating extract from *Over The Long High Wall*, one of his most important but most neglected works:

> We are now living in a society that appears – outside its propaganda and advertising – to dislike itself just as much as I dislike it. We are house-guests of the Sorcerer's Apprentice, who has let loose what he can't begin to control. What was not quite so bad yesterday will be much worse tomorrow. The past (we assume) has gone. The present is dubious and mainly unrewarding. As for the future – well, I am now an old hand at this and could be eloquent and fairly terrifying on the nightmare agenda of the world population, global pollution, vanishing natural resources, radio-active garbage, nuclear doomsday or, failing that, half-starved billions staring at endless vistas of concrete and cement – I could, but why should I? . . .
>
> Even now we have allowed ourselves to build capital cities so monstrously overgrown they are no longer manageable and civilised, wrecking human dignity and decency. Men will now plot, lie, cheat, work like demons, to buy what people used to have for nothing – quiet and a little privacy. The old are suspicious of the young; the young despise the old; and all the persons in between, at any age from thirty to sixty, are mostly busy doing something they don't particularly want to do while wondering if their life has any meaning. The happiest faces are seen in the advertiser's dreamland, inhabited by radiant beings who have just bought something.
>
> In the West we are under the spell of Admass. (I coined this term to describe a system, not the victims of it.) We are supposed to be Consumers, and not much else; surely the lowest view mankind has ever taken of itself. We are televised and advertised out of our senses. We exist among images, not realities. And hardly anybody seems to notice that quality is disap-

pearing, chiefly because so many small firms, which took a pride in what they were making and selling, have been taken over by large firms, which take pride only in their dividends. While money is more and more important, what it buys is steadily getting worse. The 'Good Life' is mostly a swindle; it should be given a bouquet – or better, a wreath – of plastic flowers. In our society everybody envies the very rich – except the people who have met them. Probably for nine-tenths of our younger people their Jerusalem or Mecca, Avalon or Garden of Hesperides, is Las Vegas, one of the stupidest, ugliest, nastiest cities on earth. We have created a society whose representative figures are politicians sold like soap flakes, and men who ask questions on television, and singers who have no voices but only a lot of hair, sweat and electronic equipment, and photographers and models. We are the supreme clever-silly people of man's history.

I don't know what you think, but I reckon that in this condemnation of later 20th century Western life, Priestley was as near the truth as anyone is likely to get.

Yet this self-same man could be transported high, high, and even higher by hope and joy. His most telling dream has often been quoted, but we must refer to it if we are to spotlight his optimism.

The dream was his "Dream of the Birds" and in it he was looking down from a lofty tower on to a multitude of wings. He remembered: "But now the gear changed and time went faster still, and it was rushing by at such a rate that the birds could not show any movement but were like an enormous plain sown with feathers. But along this plain, flickering through the bodies themselves, there now passed a sort of white flame, trembling, dancing, then hurrying on; and as soon as I saw it I knew that this flame was life itself, the very quintessence of being; and then it came to me, in a rocket-burst of ecstasy, that nothing mattered, nothing could ever matter, because nothing else was real, but this quivering and hurrying lambency of being. Birds, men or creatures not yet shaped and coloured, all were of no account except so far as this flame of life travelled through them. It left nothing to mourn over behind it; what I had thought was tragedy was mere emptiness or a shadow show; for now all feeling was caught and purified and danced on ecstatically with the white flame of life. I had never felt before such deep happiness as I knew at the end of my dream of the tower and the birds."

No place for pessimism here then; and those tempted to succumb to that black devil should refer to Dr Gortler's chastisement to another character in Priestley's Time play, *I Have Been Here Before*. Gortler exclaims: "You're like a child who thinks because it rains one morning he will never play out of doors again".

It was while playing out as a boy near his Manningham, Bradford, home that Priestley had an experience which, I am convinced, was a revelation which motivated his entire life. In *Delight* he described it this way: "I must have been about four and, on fine summer mornings, would sit in a field adjoining the house. What gave me delight then was a mysterious notion, for which I certainly could not have found words, of a Treasure. It was waiting for me either in the earth, just below the buttercups and daisies, or in the garden air . . . Morning after morning would be radiant with its promise . . . I suspect now that the Treasure was Earth itself and the light and warmth of the sunbeams; yet sometimes I fancy I have been searching for it ever since".

We must hope – and J. B. Priestley would have applauded us for doing so – that he found it. He deserved to.

CHAPTER 2: PROPHETS UNSUNG

I am a West Riding man. No amount of juggling with titles, boundaries and local government set-ups will convince me otherwise.

What am I supposed to have called myself since the reorganisation – a West Yorkshire metropolitan? They can forget that!

West Riding Bradford goes way back in history and too much of its past runs through me to justify any back-turning on the name of the area where my ancestors made their home. Without those forefathers I would not be what I am.

J. B. Priestley felt the same way. If ever there was a man who was shaped by the industrial West Riding – especially Bradford – then it was the Rebel Tyke.

He knew its faults all right (and was not thanked for pointing them out) – blemishes like its people's blunt manners, insularity, grumbling dissatisfaction, wariness of and, too often, rudeness to strangers, aggressiveness, robust vulgarity and indifference to, if not outright disdain for, the attainments of its sons and daughters finding fame in other places.

Nevertheless, Priestley relished a bevy of West Riding qualities which out-balanced the flaws – particularly when they related to Bradfordians.

As long ago as 1931, for instance, he was telling readers of the *Heaton Review*, "Bradford people are, I fancy, unusually intelligent and know about twenty times as much as they often pretend to know" – although he did note that "Bradford has offered me some of the stupidest people I have ever known".

He went on: "It has also offered me some of the very best, the kindest, the most loyal, the soundest characters. I believe that most of its citizens are romantics at heart, having a curious, glum and grumpy romanticism all of their own. It offers little or nothing to artists of any kind, but on the other hand it keeps on breeding them, doing a not ignoble export trade in them. Out of the strong comes forth sweetness. It does not surprise me that the most delicate and wistful of all modern composers, Delius, should come from a family settled in Bradford, and equally it does not surprise me that the average Bradford citizen is not at all proud of the fact. That is part of the oddity of the place and its people. What will happen to it and them, so provincial yet so cosmopolitan, so surly and yet so kind, so grim and yet so humorous? Will Bradford recover its old prosperity or will it fall gradually into decay? I don't know, and I don't believe anybody knows. All I know is that it is one of the queerest of towns and one of the most lovable".

Confirming the old saying that a prophet goes unsung in his own land, it is not unusual for cities and towns in Britain to tarry in heaping praise on their most successful sons and daughters.

But when it comes to the arts especially, Bradford often doesn't so much tarry as harry its claimants to brilliance. 'Yon's too big for his boots!" and "He ought to be brought down a peg; he needs a lesson" were, and to some extent still are, expressions typical of Bradford's abhorrence of anything lah-di-dah. It is not a commendable trait. Priestley, who said the West Riding was "a great place for discouragement" and who suffered from it, was correct about Delius; and he could have said the same about two other superbly creative Bradfordians who were to become associated with him – David Hockney and John Braine.

Delius, Priestley, Hockney and Braine "turned their backs on us" is a common assertion. That it simply isn't true counts for nothing with those who seem to believe that the highly gifted should remain tied to the apron strings of their mother city. Yet getting away from mum when you grow up doesn't mean you love her less.

Frederick Delius, who was born in 1862, six years before the birth of J.B.'s father Jonathan Priestley, was the son of a wealthy Prussian businessman who had settled in Bradford. Like Priestley he could not see his future in the local wool trade, and who could blame him with all that musical magic slumbering in him? "Father wouldn't let me be a musician and I wouldn't join the wool business, so he packed me off to Florida to grow oranges", said Delius. Nevertheless, it was the Yorkshire moors not far distant from his home during his childhood, when he was a pupil at Bradford Grammar School – the same Yorkshire moors which were to stimulate Priestley – which were to inspire some of his loveliest music.

As a man, Delius, who declared more than once "I love Bradford, even though it was a filthy place when I was a boy" (and it was), finally made his home in rural France. But even then, blind and paralysed though he had become, his character was largely Bradfordian in its tough-mindedness, outspokenness, frequent grumbling and ironic humour – the very opposite of his music.

In his outstanding film about Delius, Ken Russell made this clear. Particularly telling moments were when Deilus's wife Jelka told the young Yorkshireman Eric Fenby when he became Deilus's amanuensis (perhaps the most remarkable musical collaboration in history), "You must stand up to him"; and Fenby's assurance to Delius, "Us Tykes will pull through!"

David Hockney, who got to the heart of J. B. Priestley in his portrait of him, is an artist of genius. Work after work is radiant with light and colour – the kind of light and colour he could never have found in Bradford. The effect is stunning.

But it must have been Hockney who was stunned when repeated attempts were made by Bradfordians (frequently in letters to the local Press) to pour scorn on him and his creations. "They hurt all right", his brother Paul told me.

I'll not forget the day when a national newspaper joined the chorus of belittlement. I phoned Hockney in London, although according to that paper he had exiled himself in Paris, and I could tell by his voice that he was both perplexed and dejected. "Why can't they leave me alone?" he implored. "All I want to do is paint."

Hockney, also educated at Bradford Grammar School, has – as well as being a regular homecomer – done a great deal for his native city, especially in his work with the National Museum of Photography, Film and Television there, and his contributions to Jonathan Silver's heroic endeavours at Salt's Mill, Saltaire, where regular exhibitions comprise the world's most comprehensive displays of Hockney's artistry. They attract a multitude of viewers from a multitude of countries.

Nevertheless, many are the Bradford voices which continue to deride him, notably in contempt for the front cover Hockney designed for a local telephone directory. "Children can paint and draw just as well," they mock. Oh, that they could. If you have a copy of the directory, hold on to it. You could be glad you did one day.

John Braine, the film of whose path-finding novel, *Room At The Top* changed the whole face of British picture-making, opening as it did the gates to more honest and explicit movies, came in for many Bradford tongue-lashings for setting up home in the South in later life. They were undeserved.

Braine, a descendant of Irish immigrants, was brought up in a working-class home off Westgate, Bradford, less than two miles from where Priestley was born and reared. He went to St Bede's Grammar School before service in the Royal Navy and becoming a librarian, notably at Bingley, a place with which he soon fell in love, where he lived for a long time and where his ashes rest.

Braine wrote *Room At The Top* while a tuberculosis patient at a Grassington sanatorium and he was to find immediate fame with it. In it he made world-known Bingley Little Theatre, the Warley Theatre of his book.

It wasn't long before he also was accused of becoming "too big for his own good", especially when the film triumphed (It won Simone Signoret a best-actress Oscar). Braine was paid a mere £5,000 for that movie although it made a fortune for others.

John and I were friends for many years – right up to the time of his death during a horrific health breakdown. And I knew what a sensitive and warm-hearted man he was beneath the shell of Yorkshire grittiness he adopted. He was a Roman Catholic but his Catholicism frequently disturbed him. Like Priestley, he could recall many vivid dreams, but his dreams alarmed rather than re-assured him. He was forever dreaming that a black ship was coming to snatch him away.

One evening he had a drink too many and I had to put him to bed at our home. The black ship must have been in threatening full sail because it turned out to be a night of his groans, whimpers and cries before, half-awakening, he stumbled round the room, pulling a cabinet on to the floor with such a crash that I leaped out of bed in the next room thinking that part of the roof had fallen in.

This was the novelist who to others appeared to be a person of complete confidence when he left to make his home in the London area. Although London did attract him because of its vibrant literary and artistic community, this was not the prime reason for his departure, though.

Braine, who in his youth had, like Priestley, yearned for a cottage on or near the moors in which to hide away and write, had been told by a doctor: "John, with your medical record, and because of the money you've made, you'll be a fool not to live in a kinder climate. Thought about sunny Spain or France? If you don't fancy a place abroad, all right stay in this country. But move south man, move south. Even there the climate is much better".

On the morning John did move I was with him when a reporter from a national newspaper asked: "Why are you leaving for the south, Mr Braine? Would you call Bingley a cultural backwater?"

It was the old journalistic trick of inducing the answer desired. Braine scratched his head, considered for a moment and replied: "Well, I dunno. I suppose some might call it that".

Next morning a headline blared: "Braine calls Bingley a Cultural Backwater". Poor John, he never did live it down.

Priestley would have sympathised because he too had suffered a similar ruse.

The outcome was that he was lambasted by Bradfordians for his criticising new buildings during the heyday of the city's central redevelopment, a time when civic pride was throwing out its chest.

By chance I was there when a Fleet Street reporter asked Priestley his opinion about the buildings. I knew the reporter was pretty sure he would get the kind of answer he sought.

Priestley replied : "I don't like many of them, but then I don't like many of the new buildings of London, Birmingham and Manchester".

No mention of those other cities in next day's report, though. And no mention that there WERE some new Bradford buildings Priestley did like. What was printed was that he detested the new buildings of his hometown. Bradfordians could have strangled him.

John Braine was one of Priestley's keenest admirers and he wrote a delightful book appraising J.B.'s writings. I recall best though Braine's expansive and informative interview-article about Priestley in a 1957 issue of the *Encounter* magazine.

During the interview Braine had told J.B. "Of your plays, *Johnson Over Jordan* at the Bradford Civic Playhouse made the greatest impact on me. It marks the first time I took you seriously as a writer. One scene sticks in my mind; the dance of the office workers. There were no words used, so in a way it proved nothing about your ability as a playwright. And it proved everything, because you knew the right place for that dance, because it was an integral part of the play and not just a decoration".

Now this was the very same play and production which in 1947 was to affect me more than any play or production before or since. With O. T. Ward magnificently taking the part of Robert Johnson, the role Priestley had created for Ralph Richardson (a long and dear friend of J.B.), this 20th century morality play (with music specially written by Benjamin Britten) explored the living and the dying of an "ordinary" man before his passing into the unknown. It held me spellbound.

I shall never forget Johnson's last speech – a speech which makes nonsense of the complaint by some critics that all Priestley's writings lack any poetic power. Robert says:

> I have been a foolish, greedy and ignorant man;
> Yet I have had my time beneath the sun and stars:
> I have known the returning strength and sweetness of the seasons,

Blossom on the branch and the ripening of fruit,
The deep rest of the grass, the salt of the sea,
The frozen ecstasy of mountains . . .
But what have I done that I should have a better world,
Even though there is in me something that will not rest
Until it sees paradise. . . ?

As the final curtain fell at the Bradford Civic Playhouse, Johnson seemed transported by hope. And so was I transported – into the realisation that more than anything I wanted to make a living writing about theatre.

CHAPTER 3: EDWARDIAN TWILIGHT

Frequently I stand watching the comparatively new fountain in the decorative stretch of water between Bradford's police headquarters and City Hall – it was the much cosier-named Town Hall until "they who know best" started messing with local customs. A fine building it remains with its reaching for the sky tower, gables, open parapets and sculpture gallery of kings and queens. It was designed in the 19th century in the fashion of a Florentine building and the Victorians were rightly proud of it.

When I say I stand watching I mean I. Seldom have I noticed any other loiterer absorbing the cascading pleasure – even if the pleasure is too often marred by the empty drink cans, plastic wrappings and discarded cigarette packets chucked in the pool by litter louts.

Crowds pass by the fountain with hardly a glance. What an indifferent lot we have become. Not much seems to exhilarate us.

Yet I cannot watch the jetting spray without knowing it would have entranced J. B. Priestley.

In his collection of essays, *Delight*, he wrote about fountains. We could do worse than ponder his words. They make us aware of how much we have dulled our capacity to marvel since the short period of euphoria after the 1939-45 war.

The following is an extract from his essay:

> Fountains. I doubt if I ever saw one, even the smallest, without some tingling of delight. They enchant me in the daytime, when the sunlight ennobles their jets and sprays and turns their scattered drops into diamonds. They enchant me after dark when coloured lights are played on them, and the night rains emeralds, rubies and sapphires. And, best of all, when the last colour is whisked away, and there they are in a dazzling white glory!
>
> The richest memory I have of the Bradford Exhibition of my boyhood, better even than the waterchute or the Somali Village or the fireworks, is of the Fairy Fountain which changed colour to the waltzes of the Blue Hungarian Band, and was straight out of the Arabian Nights. And I believe my delight in these magical jets of water, the invention of which does credit to our whole human species, is shared by ninety-nine persons out of every hundred.
>
> But where are they, these fountains we love? We hunger for them and are not fed . . . Their cost is trifling compared to that of so many idiotic things we are given and do not want. Our towns are crammed with all

manner of rubbish that no people in their senses ever asked for, yet where are the fountains. . . ? Let us have fountains – more and more fountains – higher and higher fountains – fountains like wine, like blue and green fire, fountains like diamonds – and rainbows in every square. Crazy? Probably. But with hot wars and cold wars we have already tried going drearily mad. Why not try going delightfully mad? Why not stop spouting ourselves and let it be done for us by graceful fountains, exquisite fountains, beautiful fountains?

This is superb writing. Even so, if Bradford in 1994 had a dozen fountains, I doubt they would arouse much local attention after the welcoming ooohs and aaahs.

People appear too jaded by their worries and disillusionments to make time to stand and stare. For them the dream of the lasting good life has ended.

Public confidence born in the late 1940s and nurtured by the staid 1950s led to the arrogance of the insanely self-indulgent 1960s. Then came the uncertainties of the 1970s which pointed wobbily to eventual and lasting mass unemployment and deprivation – even if the hardships were to pale beside the poverty of the depression-hit 1920s and early 1930s.

A few people I saw passing the fountain had no doubt survived "very nicely thank you" after taking to heart the political philosophy which encouraged every-man-for-himself initiative. But even they, whose sleek "offices on wheels" added to the purgatory of jampacked highways, must have noted the erosion of social benevolence and communal geniality.

As for their disappointment, many of the passers-by I saw must have felt tricked by the brain-washing of years of advertisements suggesting that gorgeous homes, swanky cars, electronic wizardries and long holidays on sun-soaked beaches, heaving with bare-breasted lovelies, were not only within reach of everybody, but were everybody's by right. No wonder the throngs were not much taken by that fountain.

All their worries and disenchantment added up to a massive act of life-shrinking. And life-shrinkers were abominations to Priestley.

The mood was very different in the Bradford of his youth.

Priestley spent his early years in a city which had become the world's principal market for wool and wool products. "Bradford has never merely dealt with this place and that, but has dealt with the whole world, putting a best coat and waistcoat on the planet itself", he pointed out in 1931.

But in his youth Bradford was much, much more. It was culturally dynamic. Theatre, music, literary pursuits, sport and the visual arts thrived alongside a host of societies and organisations which catered for nearly every subject that stimulated the mind and spirit. This was in large part thanks to the expert efforts of Austrian and German businessmen (especially the German Jews) who had settled in Bradford, seeing it as a place of golden opportunity.

What's more, scores of Bradford churches, chapels and other places of worship not only gave a firm religious backbone to the city, but boosted warm friendships and an abundance of communal activities.

Bradford was as classless as you could hope for. Priestley emphasised this in 1954 when speaking at the Institute of Personnel Management conference at Harrogate.

"I remember as a boy in Bradford there were enormous differences in money matters – one man might be a millionaire and another getting his thirty shillings a week, but they still called each other 'Sam' and 'Joe', and there was no nonsense between them.

"And the men who made the money out of the muck lived with it, which was a very good thing in my view. You knew where he lived – not far from the mill – and if you disliked him you could always throw a brick through his window. There is a lot to be said for that."

Bradford, of course, did have its disgraces when Priestley was young (and, as J.B. said, its black, mucky mills). There were still too many exploited workers (and working children), too many outbreaks of disease, and too many poor people. "But there was not a lot of dire poverty; nevertheless a lot of folk had to live carefully", Priestley recalled. "But you should realise that things were cheap then and the cost of living was low".

When Priestley was a teenager, Bradford (created a county borough in 1889 and a product of the Industrial Revolution) was a city of hope, confident in its own powers and its conviction that all would get better and better, even if it had to overcome the kind of trade setbacks which had periodically bedevilled it. Priestley was to look back on the under-mining of Bradford's optimism, instigated by the 1914–18 carnage, as a time of "lost innocence".

What Priestley had experienced was actually the twilight of Edwardian self-assuredness. In realising it he was to confess to me: "I suppose I *am* an Edwardian".

He went on: "You know I have a theory that a person's formative years are not childhood as is so often maintained, but the late 'teens, say from sixteen to nineteen".

If his theory was true what did it mean for him? He was nineteen in 1913, the year before the outbreak of war and the year before, in his own words, "I grew up". "And I look on the 1914 war as the end of the Edwardian era", he said.

If J. B. Priestley was an Edwardian, his father Jonathan Priestley was very much a Victorian.

Jonathan, born in 1868, was to witness a march of progress which ultimately was to rid Bradford of a lot of the kind of misery it had suffered in the first half of the 19th century.

The first national census in 1801 showed Bradford had a population of less than 13,500. When Jonathan was three, in 1871, it had risen to nearly 146,000, with a big proportion of people working in the wool industry, although colliers abounded. Within the boundaries of the town, forty-nine mines were reported working – and coal was vital to the running of the mills.

Come the birth of J. B. Priestley and yet one more was added to the quickly growing population of more than 216,000.

For many Bradford people the first fifty years of the 1800s must have been hell on earth. Dire poverty, sickness, infirmity, near starvation, drunkenness and the dread of a horrific old age abounded in a town where working conditions were often appalling and where bare-footed exploited children in rags, stinking cellar dwellings and cheap brothels were commonplace.

No wonder there was perpetual unrest and outbursts like the 1826 riot at Horsfall's steam power loom mill in the North Wing by unemployed hand combers and weavers. Two were killed and many wounded.

As late as 1848 (but twenty years before the birth of Jonathan Priestley) conditions were still so grim that a surveyor reported: "Masses of filth in all directions, giving off foul stenches". It was so bad that medical men issued grave warnings of the danger of a cholera epidemic.

Jonathan Priestley, J.B.'s father.
(Source: Tom Priestley)

Jonathan and Emma Priestley. J.B.'s mother and father.
(Source: Tom Priestley)

White Abbey Feeding Centre, Green Lane School, 1908. Jonathan Priestley
(in suit) standing in centre. (Source: Bradford Libraries)

The year Jonathan Priestley was born indicated that changes *were* going to be made. A major scheme of central street improvements started operation, for example; the first appointment of a Smoke Inspector was made; reformative work on the sewage system was planned; and the first Bradford-made bicycle was constructed by a local boiler-maker. It was in 1868 too that the *Bradford Observer* changed from a weekly to a daily morning paper. Jonathan Priestley was to take it throughout his life, preferring it to the London papers – both under its original title and when it changed its name to the *Yorkshire Observer*, a paper for which J. B. Priestley was to write.

Jonathan Priestley, a schoolteacher, would have been quick to tell you that his mind before the birth of his only son was much troubled by the still far from satisfactory social and working conditions around him. For him it would have been unthinkable not to become a socialist – though not a socialist of the doctrinaire or Marxist kind. He was never that. The Christianity of the local chapel motivated him too much. J.B. was always proud of his father's moral courage and his sticking to what he thought right – no matter how his son argued with him. J.B. applauded his father, for instance, for denouncing the Boer War.

The young Jonathan Priestley did not fail to notice that too much poverty and too much abuse of the underprivileged still existed. He lived through too many slumps and public setbacks not to insist that something must be done – even crazy setbacks like the demand of dressmakers for pieces of a different width which caused thousands of narrow looms to be scrapped.

He witnessed the terrible 1891 strike at Manningham Mills which led to a clash between police and strikers in Town Hall Square. There was serious rioting with many injured. Eventually infantry with fixed bayonets had to form a barrier across Tyrrel Street. It is not surprising that in that very same year the first Independent Labour group in Britain was formed. It would come to be regarded as the parent of the National Independent Labour Party.

For all the public unrest, Jonathan Priestley in his younger days was to see a remarkable growth of beneficial Bradford enterprises. Only two years after Jonathan was born, for instance, W. E. Forster, MP for Bradford and Minister of Education, saw his great National Education Act passed and a Bradford School Board elected. At the time religious, factory and private schools in the town were dealing with a total of 19,000 children out of an estimated child population of 80,000.

In that 1870 year too the foundation stones of the handsome Town Hall and the new and soon flourishing Mechanics' Institute were laid; Lister

Park (where J. B. Priestley was to spend many happy hours) was bought by the Corporation and opened to the public; and the Textile Society was established.

From then and right up to the 1914–18 war there was a spate of social innovations and improvements which broadened and made more satisfying the lives of tens of thousands – thanks not infrequently to the paternalism of some manufacturers and bosses.

The Bradford of Jonathan Priestley's youth benefited also from an immense influx of immigrants seeking work and opportunities there. They came from all parts of England and especially from Ireland and Germany.

They arrived from Scotland too. Jonathan's mother, J.B.'s grandmother, was Scottish. And as many Yorkshire folk appreciate, particularly those who served alongside Scots in the Forces, the characters of the Tykes and the Jocks have much in common. J. B. Priestley's character certainly had.

It was probably not just coincidence, therefore, that the first seat of learning to honour Priestley was the University of St. Andrew's.

CHAPTER 4: JACK IN THE DALES

On the afternoon of September 11th, 1894, Jonathan Priestley was absent from his teacher's desk at Belle Vue School, Bradford.

The school's entrance was in the city's most imposing highway, Manningham Lane. Nearby were the houses of many of Bradford's prominent businessmen, while next door stood the Belle Vue Public House, a hefty Victorian edifice in whose warren of rooms many local societies, including the popular Pickwick Club, held regular meetings.

Under thin disguise, Manningham Lane of that time was later evoked in J. B. Priestley's accounts of Bruddersford, this name being an equally thin disguise for his hometown.

Manningham Lane has changed so vastly in recent years that female strippers are now daily attractions where Bradfordians once debated finer theological, political and philosophical points over their foaming tankards.

Jonathan Priestley had left the school at lunch time (or dinner time as they always called it then) to walk the two or so miles to his tiny terrace house of Yorkshire stone. There he found his pregnant wife Emma in pain.

The couple's first child was making its impatience felt, and wild horses would not have dragged Jonathan Priestley from Emma's side.

Two days later, on September 13th, neighbours smiled and nodded when hearing the arrival cries of the baby born at 34, Mannheim Road, Manningham. John Priestley had come into the world.

He was not to be known as John though. From his infancy they called him Jack Priestley, and Jack was the name used by his relatives, friends and close associates throughout his life.

Mannheim Road might have had a lower middle-class look in 1894, but it proved to have an appropriate title. One of the several streets in the area bearing Germanic names (like nearby Heidelberg Road and Bonn Road which also testified to the German influence in late 19th century Bradford), Mannheim Road was called after the ancient town lying at the convergence of the Neckar with the Rhine.

Late in the 1880s Mannheim was not only a leading commercial and industrial city, but it vibrated with artistic activities, especially drama. And baby Jack was to live to consider play-writing his finest accomp-

Copy of Priestley's birth certificate. The "B" for Boynton was added later in his life.

lishment. It proved so accomplished that the name of Priestley must have become almost as familiar to Mannheim audiences as to English ones.

Little is known about J.B.'s mother Emma. She died soon after her son was born – from cancer thought Priestley's half-sister Winnie. J.B. himself had no recollection of her, but years ago in the *Sunday Telegraph* he said he believed her to be a woman of vitality and fun who came from "the careless and raffish side of the working class, people content to live 'back o' t' mill' and to blue their money on beer, fish and chips and music halls".

34, Mannheim Road. Priestley's birth place and home until he was ten. (Source: Mabel Bruce and Bradford Libraries)

Priestley had no doubt that his father fell much in love with Emma Holt as she was called before he was married to her at St John's Baptist Chapel, Bradford, in August 1891. Yet Priestley suspected that when he was young his father was somewhat uneasy, looking out for any too carefree traits J.B. might have inherited from his mother.

Jonathan Priestley was a responsible and respectable man – and he had no time for music halls. I wish we knew what he thought of J.B.'s uncle Tom Holt who was an entertainer before keeping a pub. It is believed the Holt family was of Irish origin; and Tom Holt certainly had a puckish face typical of many in the Emerald Isle.

J. B. Priestley could not recall his mother ever being mentioned in his presence. It was as if there were "a conspiracy of silence" he said. I know exactly what he meant.

My own mother died when I was an infant and I have no memory of her. Like Jonathan Priestley, my father married again, and like J.B. I was fortunate to have one of the best step-mothers anyone could have. Nevertheless, mention of my real mother was almost non-existent. I suspect it was misplaced kindness; that they thought such talk would disturb me too much.

J. B. Priestley as a baby. (Source: Tom Priestley)

J.B. said: "Apart from dark bewilderment when I was small, I wasn't to yearn for my mother. I became aware nevertheless that there was something missing inside". I could say the same.

What subconscious effect his mother's death had on Priestley he never knew. Neither shall we. Yet it must have had an effect.

Jack Priestley was nearly four when, in August 1898, his father married again – to Amy Fletcher who worked in a confectioner's shop.

For what must have been more than three years, therefore, little Jack had only one parent. He was confused and very unhappy. But female concern was not denied him. For a time there was a housekeeper and a grandmother lived in. The only discordance he remembered was when he kicked over a can of paint and got into bother – doubtless well deserved.

His earliest memory though was of sitting on his grandfather's knee in a horse bus on a cold winter's night. "I was fascinated by the thick straw on the floor, which was there to keep people's feet warm."

Jonathan Priestley, whose father had been an overlooker at a Bradford mill and who must have sacrificed a great deal to send his son to a teacher-training college, was an excellent schoolmaster. He had strong views, however. He believed that a man should always work hard, should not fritter time on frivolities, should not tolerate meanness of spirit, should stand up both for what's right and his own rights (the National Union of Teachers must have been proud of him) and should take care of his body – he was an outstanding swimmer, a good cricketer, and an avid walker. Yet he also believed that a man shouldn't be such a po-face that he had no place for laughter – and how Jonathan Priestley would laugh when enjoying those family parties where he would lead or join in the home-made fun with the exuberance of a schoolboy.

Jonathan, who would flare with temper if he thought others were trying to take advantage, was a pillar of strength at Westgate Baptist Chapel where he gave Sunday Afternoon Brotherhood talks. Bradford came to respect him and his socialist ideals, even if a few did say he had too wide a puritanical streak.

J. B. Priestley was to make known: "I was very fond of my father. Indeed I loved him. He was unselfish, brave, honourable and public spirited. Bradford, after hearing often what he thought of it, came at last to cherish him. Though not a pious type, he was one of the most conscientious and hard working members of our Baptist chapel and Sunday school, both of which I detested at all ages. A Sabbatarian, he soon lost his temper in any argument we had about the Lord's Day".

Jonathan Priestley deserved to get on, and did. So much so that in 1904, when J.B. was ten and his half-sister Winnie nearly one, he and his family were able to move to a brand new home, 5 Saltburn Place. It too was a terrace house, but it was far more spacious and handsome than the one in Mannheim Road. What's more it had open views and fields nearby, even though it was but hundreds of yards from the previous home. Initially, the Priestley had only two Saltburn Place neighbours, the Wright and the Thompson families, each of whom had a grocery shop in North Parade, one of Bradford's best shopping streets.

Manningham, which had been a village not long before, was a salubrious suburb in those days and Saltburn Place was a "posh" address. Jonathan Priestley felt proud – even to the extent of having street trees planted, chasing off lorry drivers making a short cut, and winning a fight which, for a long time anyway, prevented other Saltburn Place houses being built. He knew too much about the legalities of the drains system.

In *The Edwardians* J.B. was to describe No 5: "It had a kitchen, where we ate when we were by ourselves; a front-room, where we ate when we had company; a smaller and gloomier back room; a bathroom on the half-landing, two bedrooms and two attics. The front attic was my bedroom from the first, and afterwards my 'den'. This house, solidly built of stone, cost about £550".

J. B. Priestley's childhood suffered considerably because of the ineptitude of an infants' teacher. "The woman I remember at Whetley Lane Primary School obviously disliked me, possibly, I fancy now, because she disliked my father who had taught once, on the junior level, at the same school", revealed Priestley in *Instead of the Trees*. "I can just recall that stupid woman's face, square and ever frowning in my direction, as I remember my own terror and despair, at an age when you don't realise that time may soon change everything, when you feel small, helpless and apparently doomed, arriving day after day with fear curdling your inside.

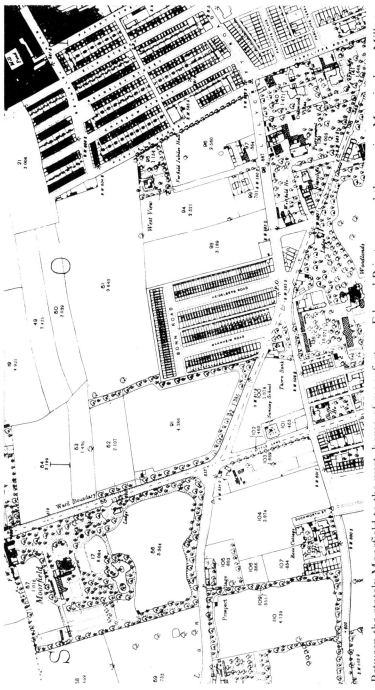

Between the stately Moorfield to the west, home of manufacturer Edward Priestman, and the massive Manningham Mills to the east, lies Mannheim Road, birth place of J. B. Priestley. (J.B.'s next home, in Saltburn Place, was shortly to be built in field number 52!) (Source: Ordnance Survey 1893)

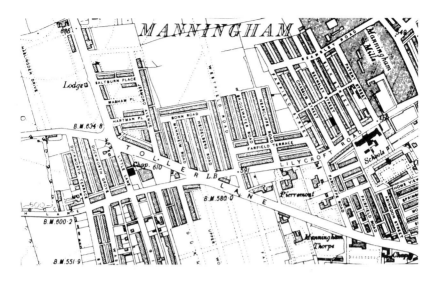

The Mannheim Road/Saltburn Place area of Bradford in 1909.
(Source: Ordnance Survey)

5, Saltburn Place. Home of Priestley from 1904.
(Source: Mabel Bruce and Bradford Libraries)

I call that woman stupid because she can't have had any imagination at all and was really unfitted to be in charge of young children".

Yet, praise be, there were precious moments of escape. "Occasionally during a holiday or on a Saturday, I would go for a walk into the country with my father, who was something of a botanist (He had many interests) and would go far afield looking for some unusual flower . . . I would be at his side for miles and miles. Our energy was prodigious".

To go walking was to remain a favourite activity throughout J.B.'s life, and some of his happiest memories of youth were of taking "a three-penny tram ride to Arcadia" as he called it. The sooty haze of Bradford was soon left behind as he reached the lush green hollow of Bingley ("The throstle nest of old England" locals named it) and made his way to the moors above nearby Eldwick. On their edge stood Dick Hudson's, "the grey old inn" he was to describe in one of his loveliest essays, and whose hefty helpings of ham and eggs J.B. was to savour mentally for the rest of his life.

In those days an unpolluted countryside was very close to Bradford, as were the wild cries of curlews and the singing of larks. We should not be surprised that in his works Priestley was to mention birds (especially larks and curlews) many times. It was testimony to the love of open spaces J.B. inherited from his father.

J.B. always regretted not having spotted a new flower for him; and as late as 1972, forty-eight years after the death of Jonathan Priestley, he was writing: "Last night rather casually I switched on the television set, which showed me quite unexpectedly a flight of birds against a tropical background, in colour that wasn't harsh or too bright and could have come out of a good painter's palette. It was all the more attractive, almost beautiful, because it was so unexpected, a gift from the blue. And how my father, a nature-lover, would have clapped his hands at it!"

It was not long after J.B.'s first acquaintance with the moors near Bradford that the rural horizon extended for him – taking in the Lake District where in the 1920s he was to share a holiday in Borrowdale with his friend Hugh Walpole, who collaborated with him in writing the novel *Farthing Hall*, and the beautiful Yorkshire Dales where he went on walking tours. For J.B., as it had been for Delius, it was over the hills and far away into some of the most magnificent countryside in Britain.

And he delighted in Dales people – characters all. He found good friends there, including Dick Chapman, a teacher in Bradford before retirement, who showed him how to catch crayfish.

When he was actually out walking, though, Priestley usually preferred to be on his own. It must have stimulated his imagination and given it full rein.

Priestley was close on sixty when he took up gouache painting (and not a bad painter he turned out to be) and the Dales acted like a magnet to him and his easel. By then, however, it was not always easy to find a suitable spot. His friend Percy Monkman, an outstanding Bradford artist and an equally outstanding actor at the Bradford Civic Playhouse, remembered: "The last time we met to paint was in Burnsall. Jack was looking for something to paint on Sunday and, of course, it was crowded. 'Not a chance', he said. We dashed off to Linton which, thankfully, was quiet and had subjects galore".

"For years, people were for ever telling me they had spotted Jack in the Dales – at Kettlewell, Arncliffe, Hubberholme, Wensley, Buckden or some such lovely place", said his half-sister Winnie whom from here on I shall call his sister. Priestley thought of her that way. Half-sister has too cold a sound to it. I know. I have a half-sister and I would not dream of calling her anything but sister.

There could have been a chance of Priestley living out his later years in the Yorkshire Dales had they not by then been too frequently cold for him – and not plagued by so many vehicles.

Priestley foresaw the coming of the misery of overcrowded roads and reeking exhausts and was not enamoured of the motor car – not since the 1920s when he had a mishap.

"I had a slow car then", he explained. "I used to change gear with a large screw-driver. But I used to get very absent-minded when driving and I hit a lamp-post in Newport, Monmouthshire. Obviously lamp-standards are sacred subjects in those parts because a large and angry crowd gathered. I thought I must give this up – so I have never driven since".

CHAPTER 5: THE BELLE VUE DAYS

Life brightened for J. B. Priestley in 1905 when, at the age of eleven, he became an elementary pupil at Belle Vue Boys' Preparatory School. He was to spend two years there before winning a place at Belle Vue High School, one of a sprinkling of higher grade schools set up by a pioneering city. By then his father had left Belle Vue to become headmaster of the new and nearby Green Lane School which was to be esteemed by posterity as the first school in the country to serve school dinners.

For young Jack the dreaded Whetley Lane infants' school had been left behind for good, and from then on he would be reasonably happy in class even if he often did get bored at his desk. Not when the subject was English or history, however. He brought to them, he said, "a great deal that I discovered for myself outside school".

What a reader he was! "He would bury his nose in the classics and could recite great chunks by heart", recalled his friend since boyhood, Percy Monkman. Jack was following in father's footsteps because Jonathan Priestley also was a voracious reader, having a special regard for Conrad.

Much credit here must go to the man who expanded and guided J.B.'s literary enthusiasm, his English teacher Richard Pendlebury. Too often the contribution a fine teacher makes to a writer's life and success is undervalued or, worse, overlooked.

Priestley was having none of that. "Richard Pendlebury was a man to whom I owe a great deal . . . who was, in the subject I have always cared most about, English, a teacher who had something like genius. I wrote many an essay for him, knowing even then that his praise and blame alike were pure gold".

Pendlebury, a tall, dark, handsome figure in stiff, high white collar, had been educated at Bradford Grammar School and St. John's Training College, Battersea, London, and was, like Priestley's father, a person who didn't believe in squandering time. He spent several school holidays, for instance, taking vacation courses in French at the universities of Geneva, Grenoble and Nancy. He joined the Belle Vue staff in 1898 and died on service in June 1918, but five months before the end of the First World War. He was forty-eight.

Priestley was to maintain that he would have escaped boredom at school if his attendance had been cut down to a couple of hours a day. "This", he explained, "is because I took so little interest in some subjects – the whole of science for a start – that I could have been better employed

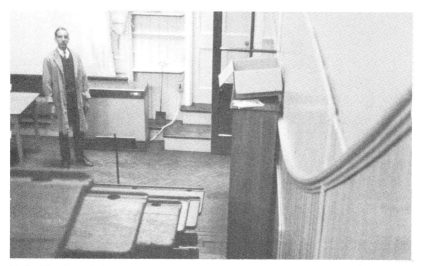

Belle Vue Boys' Grammar School, Room 12, 1968. This room was left as in Board School days so far as seating and galleries were concerned. The storage heater is, of course, more recent.
(Source: Forster Society and Bradford Libraries)

elsewhere; and that with the subjects I did care about I was so far ahead that I might as well have been sent home until the rest of the class caught up with me. Why, even with only two hours, it might have been a good idea to let me spend one of them occasionally at the girls' school next door, learning how to cook".

When Belle Vue School celebrated its jubilee in 1927, Priestley reminisced in its magazine about his time there. He said that a great question in those days was how to get to school from Toller Lane, into which Saltburn Place ran.

He wrote: "There was the Green Lane way (you turned to the left about half-way down Whetley Hill) and there was the Carlisle Road and Lumb Lane way. Some boys (and all masters) preferred Green Lane, which was certainly shorter; but I and my friends were all for the Carlisle Road way, which was twisting and turning and far more romantic.

"It is useless my attempting to describe my adventures with woodwork and ironwork, in what was to me that hateful place across the school yard. How I loathed that sawing and chiselling and filing! I always began thinking of something else at the moment when I was reaching the mark I had made on the wood, so that I went on planing or chiselling away long past the mark. And the odd thing is that if I had to do such work now, I should rather enjoy it.

"Then there was our famous singing class, consisting of throw-outs from the school choir. The part-singing of this class was a unique performance. To begin with, it had to be divided into three, as usual, and there were only about five firsts and seconds to about forty thirds or 'grunters'. And to end with, none of us could sing at all, anyhow, or we should not have been there. Nevertheless, we assembled every week in the chemical lecture room and raised the roof with 'O-oh, hush thee my-y-baby, Thy-y-sire wa-as a kni-ight'. A baby whose sire was a rhinoceros would not have accepted that as a lullaby; but we enjoyed ourselves immensely . . .

"Then what about the boys who stayed at school during the lunch hours, and so came to be called, somewhat fantastically, dinner boys; they were all barbarians from the dark and distant heights of Thackley and Wibsey, and a good many of them in my time never had any dinner at all in the school but gave themselves up to orgies of ice-cream and chocolate in Carter's sweet shop across the way? No, I could not do justice to the wild dinner boys – or the quite tame dinner itself – in less than fifty pages of print. (I once had a fight with one of them, red-haired from Idle. I had forgotten that. It would take more than fifty pages, then). The sports and games – sing heavenly muse! – would ask for epic treatment.

"I should begin with our daily scuffles in the dark sheds with little indiarubber balls, and end with our triumphs, a-glitter with cups and shields on the field of tug-of-war and football (And where now – alas – are the three medals I won, brave in silver and enamel?). I see myself floundering once more in the quagmires of Scotchman Road, better off than most because I lived not five hundred yards away, so that one last rush would carry me into a hot bath.

"And then, most important of all, the people. I dare not begin to think about the boys I walked and talked and fought with, some of whom I recognise under the disguise of worried cashiers and stout wool-buyers when I walk about Bradford these days, and some of whom (there was you, Varley, for one) I shall never see walking along any Market Street of this world. I banish their crowding faces".

But did Priestley banish them? I don't think so. He was to look back to his schooldays many times – days when he started taking notice of bonny girls, like many of the Belle Vue belles taught in the adjoining school building; and days when snowball fights took place in Manningham Lane with the lads from Bradford Grammar School.

Priestley would join in those conflicts with the gusto of a prize-fighter. Yet on some mornings of the battles he had welcomed the day with the eyes of a born writer. "The first fall of snow", he reflected, "is not only

an event but it is a magical event. You go to bed in one kind of world
and wake up to find yourself in another quite different, and if this is not
enchantment, then where is it to be found? The very stealth, the eerie
quietness, of the thing makes it more magical. If all the snow fell in one
shattering crash, awakening us in the middle of the night, the event
would be robbed of its wonder. But it flutters down, soundlessly, hour
after hour while we are asleep. Outside the closed curtains of the
bedroom, a vast transformation scene is taking place, just as if myriad
elves and brownies were at work, and we turn and yawn and stretch and
know nothing about it. And then, what an extraordinary change it is! It
is as if the house you are in had been dropped down in another continent".

During his schooldays Priestley was already trying his hand as a writer.
Yet he would never have invited being called a sissy by his classmates by
being so foolish as to wax poetical about snowfalls. "I started dozens of
school stories," he said. "I had a formula for them. They used to begin
'Hurrah, Greyfriars at last', cried Dick, or something like that. At school
I started a paper. There were the beginnings of four serial stories in the
first number, though I hadn't the slightest idea how they were going to
work out, and I wrote out one copy to be passed round. The idea was
that you could see two issues for a ha'penny. But it existed for only two
numbers, and I remember that the second was far smaller than the first".

As Jack Priestley made his way to school in his side-buttoned knee
breeches and long thick stockings (he ached for the time when he could
wear long trousers every day instead of having only the one pair
belonging to the one suit he was permitted to wear on Sundays), he must
have made envious scores of Bradford lads of his age. For those raggedly
attired boys knew they would never benefit from the kind of education
young Priestley was getting. They were half-timers, boys who worked
from dawn to noon in the mills before receiving scanty three Rs tuition in
the afternoon.

Priestley himself had to combat a lesser handicap than part-time schooling. It was a serious handicap none the less. Too much was expected of
him in some of the classrooms. He was to complain: "Those who could
not teach me would cry most unfairly, just because my father happened
to teach too, 'Well, Priestley, I'm surprised at *you*!'"

The sarcasm hurt – even if it could be put quickly out of mind once he
had stepped on to the football field. He loved football. As well as playing
full-back in school matches, he defended heroically on many West
Riding pitches (travelling to many of them by tramcar) as a member of
the Toller Lane Tykes, a team of Manningham boys.

Saltburn United football team, 1905/6 season. (Saltburn = Saltburn Place).
Priestley is in the middle of the top row. (Source: Tom Priestley)

"Sometimes we used to play twenty a side matches on the Belle Vue pitch in Scotchman Road", laughed Percy Monkman.

J.B., who in later years was to deplore the tendency by professional players to pass back the ball ("Football should be an attacking game", he insisted), once had a trial at Bradford Park Avenue. "But I wasn't very good", he told me.

"That day he might not have been", said Percy. "But Jack was a very good full-back". Priestley chipped in: "Percy wasn't bad either. Often we used to play all day long. We would go in for dinner and tea, but then it was straight back to the game".

Priestley's affection for football enabled him to write at the beginning of his *Good Companions* what must be the best evocation ever of the Saturday afternoon excitement of going to and watching a football match – before professional football became an excuse for tribal warfare among the crowds.

Here is part of it:

> For a shilling the Bruddersford United A.F.C offered you Conflict and Art; it turned you into a critic, happy in your judgement of fine points, ready in a second to estimate the worth of a well-judged pass, a run down

the touch line, a lightning shot, a clearance kick by back or goalkeeper; it turned you into a partisan, holding your breath when the ball came sailing into your own goalmouth, ecstatic when your forwards raced towards the opposite goal, elated, downcast, bitter, triumphant by turns at the fortune of your side, watching a ball shape Iliads and Odysseys for you; and what is more, it turned you into a member of a new community, all brothers together for an hour and a half, for not only you escaped from the clanking machinery of this lesser life, from work, wages, rent, doles, sick pay, insurance cards, nagging wives, ailing children, bad bosses, idle workmen, but you had escaped with most of your mates and your neighbours, with half the town, and there you were, cheering together, thumping one another on the shoulders, swopping judgements like lords of the earth, having pushed your way through a turnstile into another and altogether more splendid kind of life, hurtling with Conflict and yet passionate and beautiful in its Art. Moreover, it offered you more than a shilling's worth of material for talk during the rest of the week. A man who had missed the last home match of 't'United had to enter social life on tiptoe in Bruddersford.

J.B. knew what he was talking about. Not only had he played football himself. But he had experienced it when Bradford *did* have a fine team, especially in 1911 when Bradford City won the F.A. Cup.

Priestley left Belle Vue High School on July 31st, 1910, two months short of his sixteenth birthday. Although he had no definite plans, he had told his father that he had had enough of its niggling restraints which had knocked from him any ambition to stay on and strive for a place at a university or college.

To his astonishment, his father, yet unaware of Jack's ambition to be a full-time writer, did not explode. Instead he did what many Bradford fathers of the time did   suggest that his son find a job in a wool office. To a committed young man the wool industry offered the possibility of a rewarding career. If t'cap fitted, that was. In this case it didn't fit. It certainly didn't.

Priestley, who had played Bully Bottom in a school production of *A Midsummer Night's Dream* ("I think I have been playing Bully Bottom ever since"), had no academic honours to take with him when he finished his schooling. I have a copy of his Belle Vue record, and the space allowed for "particulars of any public examinations passed or certificates obtained while in the school" is blank. No blank has shouted out more ironically – which would have tickled Priestley. For weren't his future attainments to prove a brilliant head and sturdy shoulders above those of any other Belle Vue old boy – before or since?

CHAPTER 6: A SWAN ARCADIAN

The four years from July 1910 to August 1914, when the Great War started, were to be the most meaningful of Priestley's life as a writer. Not only did he scribble away like a youth possessed in the front attic of 5 Saltburn Place which was very much *his* room (since then it has acquired a dormer window), but until old age he was to return again and again to those years in his books, plays, essays and articles.

As he correctly pointed out in the letter I quoted at the beginning of the book, no one has ever provided better accounts of what it was like to be a youngster in pre-1914 Bradford than there are in *Margin Released* (a volume of reminiscences) and *Bright Day* (a novel about a young man growing up and learning about life and love).

What Priestley didn't say is that if it is possible to immortalise a city at a particular time then he did so to Bradford when it was at the peak of its vitality as the wool capital and a place vibrant with artistic and entertainment activities. He soon made clear to the world that "Bradford was never a music hall joke like Wigan".

Sixteen-year-old Jack Priestley did as his father suggested and got a job in the wool trade – as a shipping house clerk (a very junior one) at Helm and Company in Swan Arcade, Market Street, Bradford. He hated it.

He felt very differently about Swan Arcade. "It was no ordinary roofed-over huddle of gift shops; it was on the grand scale", he remembered. "When it opened in 1879, it was saluted as 'the most complete building of its kind in Yorkshire, if not in England'. Among English arcades it was a giant, five storeys high. The skylights were so far above my head that I hardly ever gave them a glance. I seem to remember up there an airy clutter and complication of galleries, windows, straight and curved metal supports and struts".

The office where Priestley worked (when he was not meandering round town, that is) was several floors up. Down below was the arcade's Market Street entrance which was near to where he caught his tram home. "I thought it a fine street during those years, and now, looking back, I do not believe youth and inexperience were deceiving me. Unlike the other streets in the centre of town, it was not too narrow, and it was level. Unlike them too, it had a metropolitan look, an air of massive opulence; it was a thoroughfare fit for men who would, as they said, 'cut up for a pretty penny'".

Part of the Swan Arcade photographed in 1961.
(Source: Mabel Bruce and Bradford Libraries)

When Swan Arcade was demolished in 1962 to make way for a Port-
land stone replacement block, Priestley, who more than once described
himself as a Swan Arcadian, was angry. He found such "vandalism"
incomprehensible. So, incidentally, did David Hockney who had a
brush with the developers, saying: "Swan Arcade, which was as good
as anything in Paris, has been replaced by something ugly beyond
belief".

Priestley the clerk spent a lot of time at Lyons Tea and Coffee House,
Market Street, which was a talking shop frequented not only by young
and up-and-coming woolmen but by several young newspaper reporters
whose escapades he listened to with open mouth. Yet he already knew he
would never be one of them. When it came to writing, he would tolerate
no boss – even if he was to acquire, because of many requested articles,
the journalistic discipline of meeting a deadline and writing the required
length.

J.B. said: "Sometimes on winter evenings, bound afterwards to a play or
a concert, we drank coffee and ate poached eggs at Lyons where we were
on good terms with the trio there and would persuade them not to give
us 'In The Shadows' again but try something more substantial. Once I

took one of our favourite waitresses to Shipley Glen where she would insist upon reciting bad verse to me – not a rewarding experience".

Near to Lyons was A. Briggs's tobacconist's shop where Priestley, not yet twenty, bought tobacco for his pipe – and pipe-smoking, no matter that more and more people were to call it a filthy habit, was to remain one of J.B.'s chief pleasures. However, when in company, he seldom lit his pipe without asking if there was any objection – certainly not in my presence anyway.

Briggs's was founded in 1882 and customers delighted in the little brass figure of Punch, placed inside the doorway. Punch was connected to the gas main, and its "cigarette" always had a small flame coming from it for anyone who wanted a light.

Young Priestley liked a glass of beer (who wouldn't at tuppence a pint!) and there was a good selection of pubs in or close to Market Street, like the nearby and much frequented Talbot Hotel where Branwell Brontë and his wilder cronies had more than once drunk themselves stupid during the days when he was trying to make a living as an artist in Bradford.

Even so, J.B. preferred more distant watering holes, like the Black Swan at Frizinghall and, his favourite, the ancient Spotted House opposite Lister Park, where he would meet friends from the Bradford Arts Club in Manningham Lane. "We raised our voices in argument under the low ceilings of the Spotted House; and in my book, *The Edwardians*, I described this as 'the era of hopeful debate'".

On the side of Market Street opposite to where Jack Priestley worked (or didn't) was the gothic-style Wool Exchange, the heart centre of the wool industry. Lord Palmerston had laid its foundation stone and its slender spire, 150 feet high, had a delicacy that contrasted sharply with the down-to-earth bargaining of the merchants who met there twice a week to buy and sell wool.

Scores of those men travelled the globe and many of their tales must have been overheard by Priestley whose appetite for travel must have been whetted. And a great traveller he was to become, although later he was often nervous setting out. This can be explained, I'm certain, by the bad experiences he had as a soldier during the 1914–18 war.

He sensed the romance of foreign parts, too, in some of the samples he handled at work, even if a few of them were camel hair with bits of dung still attached and, on one occasion, Chinese pigtails from Shanghai which some bright spark thought could be marketed.

The Wool Exchange (rear view) and Market Street in the 1930s.
(Source: Bradford Libraries)

He loathed his office job nevertheless. No writer could improve on his description of it in *Margin Released*. He wrote:

I was not the office boy. Low as I was, there was one even lower. At times, however, we were between office boys, and then I had to fill inkwells, put out blotting paper, uncover the typewriters, work the copying press, and take enormous bundles of samples to the General Post Office, a chore I particularly detested.

Our firm exported tops – wool that had been washed and combed and was ready to be spun into yarn – to spinners and manufacturers on the Continent. Telephoning and writing to the transport companies, railway, canal, shipping, were among my duties, not entirely a dead loss, for in those free-and-easy years, before the law interfered with pleasant trade practices, I was able to sail to Copenhagen for exactly seven-and-sixpence, to Amsterdam for about half-a-crown.

Ours was an entirely masculine office, without a touch of feminine grace and light, everything there solemn and weighing tons. A girl or two might have made a wonderful difference . . .

I had to be there at nine sharp, had an hour for lunch, but no time when I could say I had done enough and could go home. Occasionally we finished at six, more often about six-thirty, and sometimes after seven when we were given sixpence for 'tea money'.

Whatever the hour was, before leaving we had to go into the boss's private office and ask if there was anything more. Here we were out of luck. Most wool firms were bossed by men who had wives and children to return to: we had to ask permission to leave the office from the one man whose business was most of his life, who was capable of spending Christmas Day or Good Friday brooding over samples and ledgers. He may have thought he was doing us a favour, offering a last-minute rescue from the empty hours outside. But even he must have guessed that he had no hope of converting me, that every day my real life began about the time his ended.

Why I wasn't sacked after the first few months, I couldn't imagine then. I was lazy and careless: I wore what were by Bradford trade standards outlandish clothes; the time I took on any errand outside the office was monstrous, a scandal. True, I was paid very little, but even on that low rate I was bad value. Why then was I allowed to stay, never sacked, in the end taking myself off to join the army in the late summer of 1914?

I can only think now that somehow I must have represented a part of himself that this austere elderly man had repressed but not altogether destroyed, an idle, smoking, drinking, girl-chasing, verse-writing, floppy-tie-wearing self buried but still not lifeless under a mountain of wools, tops and noils. He was unlike most woolmen not only in his austere style of life but also because he was well-read. And I was often sent to a superior lending library to find a good new book for him. This was only five minutes away, but he ought to have known that I would be out of the office for the better part of an hour, enjoying my pipe – we were not allowed to smoke at work – and observing the town through an almost stupefying haze of Cut Black Cavendish . . .

One end of the office, with a broad counter, served as a sampling room; we did our clerking at the other end, which had high desks and tall narrow stools and a Dickensian air. But it lacked both the cosy comedy and the menace of Dickens, and was in fact dull. I much preferred the atmosphere of the firm's warehouse, half a mile away, where the wool arrived to be sorted.

As I went almost sliding along the greasy floor of the warehouse, dodging between the bales, I would be greeted by the sorters, caps on the backs of their heads, pipes in their mouths; and one of them might roar 'Na, lad! Ah see tha's gotten that daft bloody coat on again'. Nobody talked like that in the office, where that same coat – it was a voluminous sports jacket in a light chrome green – had met stares and murmurs of disapproval. I would have been happier, I think, working in the warehouse.

Or happier on the moors, J.B. might have added. For on some days he never returned to the office. He just took time off, and headed for the countryside.

Percy Monkman, who died aged 93 in 1986, remembered Priestley during those Swan Arcade days as "a young man wearing a Tyrolean style hat and smoking a corncob pipe". Others recalled him wearing peg-top trousers; and there were strong rumours that he spent one Yuletide with a chum at an old inn near Bradford where he smoked a church-warden pipe and tried a brew of punch. His intention was to sample Christmas very much as Dickens's Mr Pickwick would have done.

"Jack was a rebel all right", said Percy. "And an outlandish dresser then. But I never saw him without a book, under his arm or in a pocket. He was never away from the public library and the bookstalls. Nor the theatres and concert hall". Young Priestley would frequently forgo dinner, preferring to save up to buy another book. He would make do with penny buns and a gulp of cold water from a drinking fountain.

How he found the determination to write and read by gaslight well into the early hours in his attic room we can only marvel at.

"I've never been an ambitious man," Priestley once told me. "And I'd no daydreams of going to London in search of fame. My daydreams extended no farther than one day having a cottage somewhere near or on the moors where I could write away in solitude and live off a pound or two a week".

Although in later years Priestley was to go where the muse took him, and not the reverse, there was an early signal that "this writing lark" might pay off.

He was hardly out of school before he was inundating any editors whose addresses he could find with articles. And he was not yet seventeen when, to his joy, one of them was accepted and paid for by a London humorous weekly.

It was an important day in more ways than one because it opened the eyes of his father to the knowledge that his son might have some academic talent after all. "My father, not to be found wanting on such an occasion, presented me with one of his fourpenny cigars, with which, as I fancy he guessed, I had been secretly experimenting for some months", recollected Priestley.

In *Delight* Priestley recalled: "The issue of the weekly containing my article burst upon the world. Riding inside a tram from Duckworth Lane to Godwin Street, Bradford, I saw a middle-aged woman opening this very copy of the weekly, little knowing, as I made haste to tell myself, that one of its group of brilliant contributors was not two yards away. I watched her turn the pages. She came to *the* page; she hesitated; she stopped, she began to read my article. Ah – what delight! But mine, of course, not hers. And not mine for long, not more than a second, for then there settled on her face an expression I have noticed ten thousand times since, and have for years now not tried to notice – the typical expression of the reader, the audience, the customer, the patron. How shall I describe this curious look? There is in it a kind of innocence – and otherwise I think I would have stopped writing years ago – but mixed a trifle sourly with this admirable innocence is a flavouring of wariness, perhaps a touch of suspicion itself. 'Well, what have we here?' it inquired dubiously. And then the proud smirking Poet and Maker falls ten thousand feet into dubiety. So ever since that tram-ride I have never caught a glimpse of the reader, the audience, the customer, the patron, without instantly trying to wedge myself into the rocks above the black tarn of doubt. As I do this, there is the flash of a blue wing – and the bird of delight has flown".

There goes another Priestley bird!

CHAPTER 7: FULL OF HANKY-PANKY

At the time I was writing this, J.B. Priestley's sister Winnie had just reached the age of ninety. She lived in a nursing home near Salisbury where bravely she combatted the pain of arthritis and the handicap of poor sight. Sadly, she has since died.

I thought a great deal of Winnie. Like her brother, she had an exhilarating sense of fun (I enjoyed hearing her laughter) and she had no time for beating about the bush, a phrase they are particularly fond of in Yorkshire. She was forthright, straight to the point, and a stickler for fair play and fair-mindedness.

When I last spoke to her she reminisced about her childhood days at Saltburn Place where J.B., more than nine years her senior, used to tease her by calling her Fatty. "I have to confess I was rather plump", she chuckled.

She loved her big brother Jack and has particularly happy memories of those Saturday mornings when he, she and their father would go into town to Kirkgate Market (a vast Victorian building, packed with stalls, tiny cafes and cosy shopping alcoves) where they would smack their lips over the steaming pies and peas. Afterwards, if it was winter, they would toast their toes over the heating from the floor gratings.

Winnie said: "Jack was a great music lover – he knew a lot about music – and he loved to go round the music shops in Kirkgate and Darley Street. He bought a gramophone with the money he made from his first article, and he was the first to introduce me to good music, particularly Brahms whose music I love above all.

"Poor mother, though. Father had a temper, Jack had a temper and I had a temper. Sometimes the three of us would sit there glowering in defiance seeing who was going to give in first. Mother must have despaired".

The shopgirl who had been Amy Fletcher before marrying Jonathan Priestley and becoming Jack's stepmother and Winine's mother, must have been an exceptional person. J.B. described her as gentle, kind and loving, and he obviously thought the world of her. She died in August 1935.

"In certain ways mother was better to Jack than to me, letting him get away with it, no matter what" said Winnie. "She called him a gee-nius!

Darley Street with the exterior of Kirkgate Market on the left. 1891.
(Source: Bradford Libraries)

She did drill us both in courtesies, though. For example, if someone gave us something, mother was very fussy about it, demanding 'And what do you say? You say thank you'".

By telling me this, Winnie unwittingly revealed what was behind a letter I received from J.B. when I was much younger. At his request I had done a little research for him. To my complete surprise he sent me with his gratitude a signed first edition of his novel *Lost Empires*. I replied that there had been no need to thank me so generously for what, after all, was far from an onerous task. Straight back came a letter pointing out with typical Priestley bluntness that no one was ever too big to express thanks. "Thanks should always be given when thanks are due. Remember that young man", he urged. I have not forgotten his words.

Winnie, who said that her brother had "an uncanny knack of finding out about people's characters", recalled with glee the parties for family and friends (many of them school teachers) which her father relished giving at No. 5. He joined the revelries with gusto.

"Jack", continued Winnie, adored family clowning. He played the piano too; and quite a number of the guests fancied themselves as solo singers. Full of false modesty, they would turn up with music surreptitiously tucked in their pockets. 'Well, I dunno about singing a song; but go on, I'll have a try; by chance I do have a copy with me of a song I like', was the kind of response to requests. They were songs like *Watchman, What of the Night?* and ballads like that".

One of those songs (a favourite of his) would tempt J.B. to attempt singing basso profundo as he slowly drawled out: "Many a brave heart is asleep in the deep, so beware, BEE-WARE!"

They were wonderful characters at those parties, and young Jack knew it. They proved part inspiration for some of his best and most affectionate comic creations – even if some critics were to belittle them as outright caricatures. They were not.

"Jack", said Winnie, "would often have the whole family rocking with laughter as he impersonated and told us about people we knew and he had met. He knew exactly what he was doing – but he would never do it in their presence. There was no harm in him.

"In later years Jack was always good to old friends and to friends of our parents. There was Walter Holmes, I remember. We called him uncle Walter and he used to take Jack to cricket matches. He was a grand old man. Late in life, he was diddled out of all his money. It was dreadful. He ended up in lodgings, living in a very poor way. Jack used to go see him. I'm sure he gave him money".

Priestley's fondness for leg-pulling never deserted him, as Winnie could well testify. Like her father, she became a schoolteacher. She married Paul Scott, an artist, and for some years they lived at Crosshills between Keighley and Skipton. There they had a shop specialising in quality goods.

"One day Jack phoned us and announced brusquely, 'I'm coming up for Sunday dinner'. Now as every woman knows, you can make Yorkshire pudding every week-end of the year and fifty-one times out of fifty-two it comes out fine. That Sunday was the exception. 'You're pudding hasn't risen', teased Jack with a poker face. By Monday it was all round the village. I was mortified'.

Regarding the pudding of Yorkshire, Priestley would chuckle at the memory of one of his trips to the Dales. He was staying at a small inn where there was an outdoor privy. It was a lovely, sunny morning and all seemed right with the world as he sat there having a contemplative smoke. Suddenly, two feet appeared in the space at the bottom of the door and the voice of his hostess inquired: " 'Ow dusta like thi Yorkshire pudding, Mr Priestley? With or withart onion gravy?' "

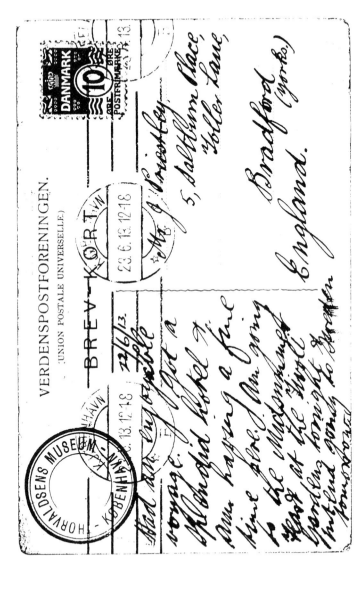

Postcard from Copenhagen in J. B. Priestley's handwriting, June 1913.
(Source: Tom Priestley)

"When he was a lad, Jack could be very moody", Winnie remembered. "He was like that at some of those family parties. Mother would go in fear and trembling of what he would do next. Yet looking back, I guess he was tormented at the time, was carrying too much in his head, was too full of ideas".

Priestley was to explain later that he could never be happy to order – like the boy in the old joke who was seen on the promenade at Morecambe being slapped repeatedly by his mother while she shouted: "When I bring thi out to enjoy thissen, tha'll bloody well enjoy thissen!"

People in the Saltburn Place and Toller Lane district were baffled by young Priestley with his "hoity-toity notions" and in his fancy clothes. "He's too full of hanky-panky", some decided. Winnie remembered how women would stop her mother when she was shopping and ask: "What are you going to do with that lad of yours?" Father had to run the gauntlet too. Neighbours would inquire of him: "Whatever are you going to make of your Jack, Mr Priestley?" It must have distressed Jonathan who believed very much in keeping up the appearance of suburban respectability.

"I'm still sorry that father didn't live long enough to see how revered a writer Jack became", said Winnie. "He would have been very proud".

Jonathan Priestley died in 1924 aged 56. He had stomach cancer but, mercifully, never knew it. He merely lost weight and with it his memory and mental alertness.

His mind was certainly agile though during those long ago years when the Priestleys prepared to go on family holiday. "Father saw to it that we had good holidays", explained Winnie. "But like a typical socialist he did it cheaply by arranging that we cater for ourselves. By this means, however, we were able to go to such faraway places as Bournemouth when nearly every other family was going to Morecambe or Blackpool. When we were there we walked everywhere; mile after mile, day after day.

"Before setting off on holiday it was pandemonium, with trunks being sent by cart to the station and father frequently losing his temper. Mind you, so did I. I could be very awkward. I remember coming downstairs with a doll and father shouting, 'You're not taking that on holiday'. I said, 'I am, or I won't go'. He said, 'You're not taking it' and I said, I am'. And so it went on.

Did Winnie take her doll? "No way!", she laughed – "and I did go on holiday".

In *Particular Pleasures* J. B. Priestley paid tribute to the acting abilities of Dame Edith Evans and, as an aside, mentioned that she had been a friend of his parents. What he didn't say was that the friendship went back to one of those Priestley south coast holidays.

"Edith was a young milliner then and was staying at the same place as we were", recalled Winnie. "Father was a strong swimmer and so was she. Each morning they went out together for a swim. I couldn't go with them because I couldn't swim. Father was rather cold to me about this. Yet he never tried to teach me.

"Mother and father became so friendly with Edith that later, when she was appearing in *The Late Christopher Bean* in Leeds, she came to visit mother. She was about to open a bazaar and she took mother along. Edith insisted she sit with her on the platform – to mother's horror because she was a very shy person.

"Years later", went on Winnie, "Edith had a flat near Jack's in London's Albany. He was always giving parties there. He loved them. And he always invited Edith Evans. Yet not once did she invite him back. This made me cross. I was at one of the parties and Edith was there as usual. Jack came up to me and whispered, 'If you want to tell her off, Winnie, you go tell her off!' "

Lister Park bandstand about 1914. (Source: Bradford Libraries)

When her brother went to make his living in London in the 1920s it was not as John Priestley. Nor was it as Jack Priestley. It was as John Boynton Priestley.

Why did he adopt that middle name? Even Winnie was not totally sure. Priestley himself was to maintain the reason went back to his youth in Saltburn Place where letters would arrive addressed to Mr J. Priestley. Did it mean they were for him or for his father? The confusion (especially if girls were writing to youthful Jack) caused some irritation, he said. So he talked it over with his stepmother and they decided he should take a name from her side of the family – that of Boynton.

But is this the full answer? The name J. B. Priestley probably seemed that it would be more arresting if it appeared on a book or an article. Much more than Jack Priestley or, merely, J. Priestley. Such reasoning most likely.influenced the choice. But we'll never really know.

When Priestley left home, the attic room which had been his private world became Winnie's. There, in a cigar-box, she found the head of a ventriloquist's doll. Her brother had bought it from a shop in Lumb Lane when Lumb Lane was a spotless working-class road, where every house doorstep was scrubbed and white or yellow donkey-stoned at the edges and where lace curtains were immaculate behind every polished window. In the 1980s the lane was to become nationally notorious, the painted dolls more likely to be discovered there then being of the kind often hustled into police vans.

The head found by Winnie had once been one of her brother's most prized possessions. In a little essay he remembered it this way:

> I was somewhere in my middle teens and I was walking along Lumb Lane, Manningham, Bradford, and for the first time ever I came to a halt outside the secondhand furniture shop there. Not only did I stop but I stared in amazement. In place of the usual Victorian junk, its window was filled with ventriloquists' dummies, all staring back at me. I bought one of the cheapest of them, with no body, just a head with its various strings . . . Ventriloquial acts continued to fascinate me, as they do to this day. It is not the jokes I care about, for they are not often very good jokes; it is the dummies. The truth is, after the first minute or two I no longer regard them as puppets manipulated by the ventriloquist. They seem to me to have a life of their own. It is a life different from ours, for I feel they belong to some gnomish race, in touch with us only intermittently, and always exasperated and indignant at our lack of understanding, their bold and roving eyes appearing to glitter with fury, their strange voices rising in protest or deepening into despair.

"Jack used to make outfits for the dummy he bought and he tried his hand at ventriloquism" revealed Winnie. "But he was not very good. He was interested in everything, though. His enthusiasm was boundless. He would have a go at most things – as long as they weren't mechanical. He was hopeless then".

When at Saltburn Place, J.B. had fleeting thoughts of becoming a musician or an actor. "It must be understood I hadn't *'Hamlet'* or *'King Lear'* in mind", he once explained. "I merely thought about going on the stage. (When at parties I amused girls of my age, they were always saying, 'You ought to be on the stage'). I saw myself as some sort of comedian, perhaps for the next few years a 'light comedian', the type that sang chorus songs about the seaside. And indeed I actually bashed out a song about the seaside one night in the Bradford Mechanics' Institute. The impresario, if he deserves such a title, must have advertised for local artistes; and I can just remember being interviewed by a fruity old character, who, after solemnly feeling my bumps, like a phrenologist, engaged me for one performance and offered me a guinea – not a bad fee in those days for a teenager".

As for Priestley's powers (or lack of them) as a pianist, they were well remembered by Dorothy M. Fieldsend, a former teacher at Carlton and Bolling schools who, in 1973, gave this illuminating account:

> I was closely associated with the now defunct Bradford Playgoers' Society (as indeed was J.B. at one time) and in the early summer of 1914 took part with other members in an open-air performance of *As You Like It*, given in the grounds of Esholt Hall.
>
> One of my fellow performers later invited me to a pleasant evening at her home in Heaton, also inviting two other of her friends to join us later. I understood they were both interested in music, literature and the theatre. They were first going for a tramp across the moors.
>
> My first introduction to Jack Priestley, then about 20, showed a stocky young man, hatless (then considered to be very unconventional), with thick black hair, shining with raindrops.
>
> An English summer was as inconsistent then as now! His friend, a kindred spirit, had opened a book shop in what is now New Kirkgate – a place for those with Leftish tendencies to browse. We passed the evening in conversation about our various activities, but one incident still remains vividly with me.
>
> Suddenly J.B. turned to me. 'You're interested in music, aren't you?' (I was music mistress at one of the local higher grade girls' schools and a member of the Bradford Festival Choral Society). 'Do you know McDowell's To a Wild Rose?' he asked. Deflatedly I had to admit my complete ignorance of this American composer. Whereupon he sat down at the piano and proceeded to play it for me. He was not a very good pianist.
>
> Years later I read in one of his early essays his statement that the true

musicians whom Beethoven would recognise in the Great Hereafter are those who, like himself and so many of us, struggle and stumble through a jungle of notes, black and white keys, sharps, flats and naturals, admitting no defeat.

I felt very dejected for the rest of the evening. The very next day I dashed off to dear old Fred Power's stall in Kirkgate Market and bought two collections, not only To a Wild Rose, but also the Sea Picture of the Voyage of the Pilgrim Fathers with the great hymn rising above the surging Atlantic billows!

The Kirkgate Market stall mentioned by Dorothy Fieldsend was for donkey's years a treasure chest for bookworms, a bumper source of sheet music for addicts of popular songs, and a delight to the general browser. It was a place of atmospheric fascination. As well as J.B., Yorkshire writer Thomas Armstrong was a frequent caller. So too was a Bradford Grammar School boy who particularly appreciated the variety and service of its second-hand volumes. He was young Francis Durbridge who went on to create the famous radio detective Paul Temple.

For more than 50 years Fred Power, who died aged 88 in 1959, was the proprietor. He had been associated with the business long before then, however, for his father, Robert Power, had started it in 1872.

Fred's fondness for cigars was as much a characteristic as his wide knowledge of the book trade. He stocked books to meet all tastes and all purses.

Years ago, Fred was involved in a friendly tiff with J.B. who, in his *English Journey*, made certain remarks about a certain bookstall. Following correspondence, Priestley visited Fred and was shown round the storerooms upstairs. There Fred pointed out that some of the books of which Priestley had been critical were, in fact, written by an author whose initials were J.B.P.

Months later on a flyleaf of the Everyman edition of Priestley's *Angel Pavement* appeared a note of commendation of Fred Power's authority on books in general.

There wasn't a trace of the old hanky-panky when J.B. made this decision. He knew he had been wrong about Fred's storerooms; and with typical honesty he confessed it – in a most generous and public fashion.

CHAPTER 8: THOSE DREADED SUNDAY NIGHTS

With all his writing J. B. Priestley drove himself so arduously that he came to think he might be propelled subconsciously by the puritan ethos of faith in the saving power of work.

Although he was very seldom a man who worried, he sounded rueful when he said: "During the 1930s and 40s a lot of ill will came my way. Friends said this was envy but I think it was largely of my own doing. Almost always I was driving myself too hard, pursuing two or three careers at the same time. I was never really arrogant. Arrogance is not one of my failings; but may have appeared to be simply because I was extremely impatient".

In 1954 J.B. told the 300 guests at a celebration at the Dorchester Hotel, London, to mark his sixtieth birthday: "Although I have been praised for my industry, I would have preferred to work less hard, but better".

But could he have worked less hard even if he had wanted? I doubt it. "Daddy's like a pressure cooker; if you tried to stop him writing I think he'd blow up", observed one of his daughters.

On one occasion Priestley declared: "People sometimes ask me if I worry about death. The answer is: Not at all. But I'd be furious if it interrupted me while I was in the middle of working out an idea".

Why did he push himself so fiercely? For the answer we must, I think, look back to 5 Saltburn Place and his father. Although a teenage J.B. not infrequently argued and occasionally rowed with his dad, and came near to defying him over the matters of his constant theatregoing and his choice of some young cronies, Jack had too much affection and respect for his father not to be influenced by some of his parent's beliefs. High among them was his father's conviction that hard work engendered moral strength.

"My father was not exactly a puritan", J.B. pointed out. "But there was a puritanical streak in him. He liked going to concerts (and Bradford was very musical in those days), but rarely went to the theatre, and only under great pressure, when frivolous relatives from London descended upon us, consented to visit a music hall. Most entertainment seemed to him immoral, not so much because he thought it bawdy or vulgar but because it seemed to him to waste time and money and attention that ought to be given to more serious things".

Much of Jonathan Priestley's attention was divided between socialist activities (he was proud of knowing fellow Bradfordian Fred Jowett who contributed so strongly to the forward march of British socialism) and Westgate Baptist Chapel which the young J.B. had to attend at least twice every Sunday – for morning service and for Sunday school in the afternoon. They still called Sunday the Sabbath then and Jonathan Priestley was almost a fanatical Sabbatarian to whom Sunday displays of any type of public levity were offensive. His Scottish ancestors on his mother's side would probably have been proud of him – and indeed he did have the looks of many a Scot. J.B. described him as "stocky, round-headed, red-faced, with bright blue eyes, fair hair and gingerish moustache" – in appearance hardly at all like his son.

You can take a thinking youngster to the water of sectarian religion but you cannot make him gulp it down. In that chapel Jack Priestley was already surveying and questioning a dogmatic doctrine. The rebel in him was in action.

He remembered: "As a boy sitting in chapel in my best suit, I did no worshipping at all, was visited by no emotion but felt detached from all the proceedings. Our dourest parsons, who followed the nonconformist fashion of long extemporary prayers, always seemed to me to be bent on bullying God. After a few *Beseech Thees* as a mere politeness, they adopted a sterner tone and told Him what they expected from Him and more than hinted He must attend to His work. What might be all right long ago in the Near East, to which we sometimes confusingly returned, would not do for Bradford in 1905. And the hymns, to which I occasionally lent a voice, seemed to me either grim or idiotic".

For Jack Priestley, the chapel during the week was a very different place, and one which must have nourished his writer's love of West Riding characters and their socialising. The main room of the Sunday school, he explained, was fairly large and had a number of useful classrooms. During the week "these crackled or hummed with life many a day and most evenings".

"There were sewing meetings, gymnastic classes for young men, teas-and-concerts, lantern lectures, conjuring entertainments, and best of all, the bazaars which kept people happily busy for weeks and weeks and were then uproarious affairs for three or four nights, during which I promoted myself into being announcer and 'barker' for the various entertainments. At the same time the regular chapelgoers created their own little circles of friends, who invited one another to magnificent high teas (with rum out of 'a little brown jug') and then played whist, always leading their aces, or sang drawing-room ballads – I accompanied dozens of them.

"Nowadays we are asked to listen to the desperate cries of the lonely. It seems that in our many-towered cities there are decent people eating their hearts out with loneliness. I tell you, anybody who regularly attended Westgate Baptist Chapel, Manningham, Bradford, when I was a boy there, never suffered from this affliction".

In *Outcries and Asides* Priestley provided a superb evocation of what Whitsuntide was like in the Bradford of his youth. Anyone my age or older can remember, as J.B. did, having to wear those new Whit clothes – if your parents could afford them or, if you were a girl, make them – and receiving a brand new penny that some kind of relative tucked in your pocket. With shining shoes and shining faces we went forth like an angelic brigade — in appearance anyway.

Priestley lamented: "The disappearance of Whitsuntide must astonish or sadden anybody who was young in the North when I was. In our time, Whitsuntide ranked next to Christmas. It was far more important than Easter, which came too early in the North, so that when I think of Good Fridays I only recall trying to shelter from sleet on the moors. One might also say that it was not until about Whitsuntide that the sun came out there. But when it did come out, we offered it something to admire, for it was on Whit Sunday that we all wore our new clothes – rather stiffly if we were self-conscious boys and youths. After I turned sixteen and went roaring out into the world, I chose my own clothes, not without colour and some wild free cuts, alarming and disgusting my father, who wore a frockcoat on Sundays and at all times was anxious not to startle the neighbours. But in my earliest teens I was still in sober worsteds and serges and took no pride whatever in them because they were new.

Mrs Amy Priestley, J.B.'s step mother, in 1936.
(Source: Tom Priestley)

"Whit Monday was the day set aside for Sunday school 'treats', as we always called them. If the chosen fields were distant, we were transported there in cleaned-up coal carts, which to this hour I associate with Bradford beanfeasting. Once there, we ran races – flat, three-legged or egg-and-spoon – and were given mugs of tea and large flattish buns. We lads of thirteen or fourteen let steam off and greeted the dawn of sex by chasing the girls of our age round the outskirts of the field, which was always of a fair size. The girls giggled, screamed, and then said 'It isn't fair' when they were caught. All we did when we caught them was to let them go; we had not yet arrived then at any nymph-and-satyr business, though probably all that chasing and screaming, with so many girls, often quite fleet of foot, allowing themselves to be caught and shaking their curls at us as they cried it wasn't fair, represented an archetypal sexual game. But though not without stirrings of sex, I think what chiefly appealed to us lads was the chance of letting loose our almost insane stores of energy, and doing it in an unofficial and rather disreputable fashion – and never mind the silly races, which many of us had to be bullied into running.

"What did not appeal to us – at least never to me – were the dominant personalities of these organised 'treats', usually either Sunday school superintendents or the more active deacons. They were determinedly cheery and jolly with an undercurrent, soon reached, of bullying and disapproval. It is a type I heartily disliked then and have never cared for, have regarded with suspicion, ever since. Even so, these were good days, returning us exhausted, full of buns, and with the smell of early June grass still pleasantly haunting us. Incidentally, we were not allowed to wear our best new suits, with which we had gone on parade the day before".

As he grew out of his boyhood outfits, Sunday evenings in Bradford became especially dreaded by Priestley. If he didn't go to evening chapel there was nothing for him to do apart from roam round town like scores of other lads, buy cups of tea and eye the attractive, but equally frustrated, girls. Hardly any organisation held a meeting and there was no public entertainment – and it was to remain like that for many years. Like Priestley, many of my generation, after being packed off to church two or three times each Sunday, despaired – until, at last, the cinemas were allowed to open on Sunday nights. There had been so many objections to this by older people, you would have thought picturehouses were haunts of the devil. Some of the hottest arguments between J.B. and his father were about the "rights and wrongs" of doing nothing on a Sunday evening.

In the early 1930s, Priestley made one of his frequent returns to Bradford. By chance it was a Sunday evening and he noted that nothing had changed for young people. "I explored all the centre of the city and discovered that there were one or two very small cafes open and then, from seven o'clock onwards, all the pubs, and nothing else", he wrote in his *English Journey*. "You could take your choice and either promenade up and down Darley Street, North Parade, Manningham Lane, or go into the nearest pub. Ever since I remember, elderly citizens have been protesting against this practice of promenading on Sunday nights. They have always been disgusted by the sight of young people monkey-parading in this fashion. It is, however, these same elderly citizens who have seen to it that nearly all doors leading out of the street shall be locked against these young people. They cannot listen to plays or music, cannot see films, cannot even sit in big pleasant rooms and look at one another; so they walk up and down the street".

By his late teens, Jack Priestley had become addicted to the pleasures his father frowned upon most – visits to the straight theatre and (delight, delight) to the music halls.

Jonathan Priestley did not object to, in fact he encouraged, his son's attendance at the orchestral concerts at St. George's Hall, Bradford, where Jack found bliss in the music of, among others, Brahms, Bruckner and Elgar ("What is this deep Englishness that enchants fellow countrymen like myself?" J.B. was to ask about the works of the master of the Malvern Hills. "It is easy to recognise and enjoy but hard to explain".)

But Jack's visits to the plays at the city's Theatre Royal (where top productions from London were often staged) and the Prince's Theatre (melodramas were its speciality), and his even more frequent visits to the Empire and Palace music halls, were a different matter altogether. Jonathan Priestley's temper flared again and again. There was no stopping Jack, however.

We must be grateful there wasn't. "My father must have felt I had inherited from my mother's side a want of respect for serious things and an unquenchable thirst for amusement", declared Priestley. "What he never could have guessed, what I did not know myself until some years after his death, was that my constant and not uncritical attendance at theatres and music halls (then perhaps at their best) during that formative time, was preparing me for a future career as a dramatist.

"He must have been in despair when he learned, as he had to in the end, that all too often I played truant from night school lessons in advanced commercial French and German (and what an agony of boredom *they* were!) to attend the first house at the Empire or Palace. And he did not live long enough to learn that I was in fact not idling my future away but busy indeed with my education. For though I never wrote the kind of thing they were performing at the Empire or Palace, I believe I learned from this hard school of entertainment certain matters – for example, economy, timing, the relation between stage and audience – later to be of the utmost value to me. The ideas may not have been there, but much of the fundamental craft was; and the fourpences I paid to sit, jammed and half-suffocating, in the balcony of the Empire were not money wasted. It was the shillings demanded for those agonising hours of commercial French and German that brought no return. But how could my father have guessed that?"

Priestley went on: "There were times when my father's exasperation boiled into anger. Usually this happened when he contrasted my behaviour with that of some young prig, the son of a neighbour, who was known to be toiling day and night to perfect himself for the wool trade. I could not help jeeringly dismissing these lads, whom I knew to be spiritless twerps; and then my father would roar: 'He'll be a man when you're a monkey!' Where this hard saying came from, I never knew, but I always heard it unabashed".

The Empire music hall (almost opposite where the now spectacularly renovated Alhambra Theatre first opened in March 1914, a few months before Priestley went to the war) was a good few cuts above the Palace in its quality of programmes. It could have been, and possibly was, a model for one of those entertainment palaces J.B. brought to life so vividly in his novel *Lost Empires*. The Bradford Empire had Priestley's favourite boards. Upon them performed a host of lustrous artistes, including the young Charles Chaplin, W. C. Fields (then a comic juggler), Marie Lloyd, Grock the clown, George Formby senior and Little Tich about whom, in *The Balconinny*, Priestley wrote a captivating essay.

His favourite among the comedians, however, was Jimmy Learmouth. J.B. informed his readers: "He was still, I think, a youngish man when he died. He never became a West End star and was, I fancy, unknown in London, though provincial audiences adored him . . . If I rule out two or three great international clowns, then Jimmy Learmouth was the funniest man I ever saw . . . Like all great comics he didn't make jokes, he was himself one huge joke".

When Priestley was eleven years old, the Theatre Royal in Manningham Lane became world renowned (or notorious, some said) because it presented the very last appearance anywhere of Sir Henry Irving. On Friday the thirteenth of October, 1905, he was taken ill while starring in Tennyson's *Becket* and died that same night in the foyer of the Midland Hotel, Bradford.

That Irving should have chosen to appear at the Theatre Royal underlines what a quality theatre it was. West End stars acted there regularly.

Priestley saw many of them, often thanks to his friend Seth Boothroyd of Heaton, Bradford, who had a pass.

Jack and Seth had been in the same form at Belle Vue school and they often walked there together from Toller Lane. When in 1964 Priestley was asked and agreed to open formally the new Belle Vue school building, off Bingley Road, it was Seth who wrote the letter of invitation. He was then vice-president of the Belle Vue Old Boys' Association.

The Theatre Royal meant a great deal to J.B. – not only because of its plays, but because of its lavish pantomimes, one of which was to hold particular significance for him as I shall tell later.

His visits to the Royal gave him an "in" to writing about the cultural life of Bradford in the *Bradford Pioneer*, a Labour journal. Very soon he was contributing to it not socialist articles but a weekly personal column called Round the Hearth in which he reviewed artistic activities. It was so personal that the editor informed readers: "It must be distinctly understood that Round the Hearth is pre-eminently a personal feature so that the opinions expressed therein are not necessarily those of the paper itself". Personal or not, his writing of the column gave him free access to Bradford theatres – and, to his joy, Bradford music halls.

It was his visits to the Theatre Royal before these "illustrious" columnist days, which allowed Priestley to write one of the best descriptive pieces about what it was like to wait outside a theatre in Edwardian times. He reflected:

"When I was a lad and regularly took up my place in the queue for the early doors of the gallery in the old Theatre Royal, Bradford, the actors on their way to the stage door had to walk past us. I observed them with delight. In those days actors looked like actors and like nothing else on earth. There was no mistaking them for wool merchants, shipping clerks, and deacons of Baptist chapels, all those familiar figures of my boyhood. They wore suits of startling check pattern, outrageous ties, and preposterous overcoats reaching down to their ankles. They never seemed to remove all their make-up as actors do now, and always had a rim of blue-black round their eyelids. They did not belong to our world and never for a moment pretended to belong to it. They swept past us, fantastically overcoated, with trilbies perched raffishly on brilliantined curls, talking of incredible matters in high tones, merely casting a few sparkling glances – all the more sparkling because of that blue-black – in our direction; and then vanished through the stage door, to reappear, but out of all recognition, in the wigs and knee-breeches of 'David Garrick' or 'The Only Way'. And my young heart, as innocent as an egg, went out to these romantic beings; and perhaps it was then, although I have no recollection of it, that the desire was born in me to write one day for the Theatre".

CHAPTER 9: BOOTS IN GIBBET LANE

If the young Priestley dreaded Sunday evenings, he didn't feel much happier about Mondays in Saltburn Place.

During a BBC Home Service broadcast in June 1943 he told listeners:

"When days really were days and each had a character of its own, when I was a boy up Toller Lane, Bradford, there was no mistaking Monday. You could even smell it, just as you could Thursday, which was baking day in our house. Monday of course was washing day. It was a day when the house was fairly lost in soapsuds and steam.

"It was a day when mothers and wives and sisters were very busy and apt to be short-tempered. Menfolk were there only on suffrance, and if they had any sense, and didn't want to be reminded of all their various weaknesses by irate females, they crept about the house carefully, avoiding the baskets of wet clothes and the rickety clothes horses near every fire. And for that matter you had to creep into the house rather carefully, negotiating the lines of washing in the backyard.

"Sometimes you had to go down into the steam cellar and turn the creaking, groaning mangle. I can still remember being very little and staring up at the mangle and seeing it as a vast mysterious machine. But among this tremendous female business of rubbing and wringing out and mangling and hanging out to dry, in this almost tropical atmosphere of steam and soapsuds, lit with lighting flashes of feminine irritability, the comfort-loving and gluttonous male had a poor day of it.

"The house was cheerless and without welcome. The meals, when they arrived – and they had a trick of arriving late and being fairly flung at you – were apt to be both meagre and monotonous; scrag ends of cold mutton or brisket escaping from its string and looking the shadow of its Sunday self; melancholy cabbage and potatoes done anyhow; bits of fruit pie with the lumpy residue of Sunday's custard. No pleasure in eating. And no visitors that day, no fun. You lent a hand with the job or kept well out of the way. It was Monday and the washing had to be done".

What could be called THE dreariest and most ominous Monday like day of Priestley's life, the day when it was hinted to him and millions of others that the biggest human mangling and clean-up operation known was underway, dawned in August 1914 when the British Empire went to war with Germany.

The rest of the family being at the seaside, Priestley was alone in the house – a house generally bustling with friends and neighbours "just popping in for two minutes" – when the shouts of the newsboys were to be heard in every street. In a month he would be twenty.

He said much later that he did not know why he enlisted. Certainly it was not because of any patriotic fervour. Quite likely, he agreed, it might be because he sensed the world would never be the same, that his Market Street days were over and it was time to march on.

By early September, therefore, he found himself an infantry soldier with the Dirty Dukes – the Duke of Wellington's West Riding Regiment – at their depot in Halifax. For some days he was allowed to go home at night to sleep, on condition he was back first thing next morning. "I clomped in boots that seemed to weigh a ton to and from those barracks in Gibbet Lane. That was a fine start for my war – Gibbet Lane!"

J.B.'s first unsavoury taste of Army life, or rather non-taste thank you, was of being ordered by the sergeant major to scrape fat out of old cooking tins. He bristled at the NCO's favourite command, "Hey – you!"

Even greasy tins gave way all too quickly to the mud of trench warfare. Eventually the regiment took over Vimy Ridge and Souchez from the French. Then, in 1916, J.B. was wounded, partly deafened and buried deep in earth by a large trench mortar. One soldier near him was killed.

Lance-corporal Priestley, as he had now become, was sent back to England to hospital. After convalescence and training in Wales, he was given a commission as a junior officer with the Devon Regiment. He returned to the front where, in the summer of 1918, he was gassed during an attack. It was off to hospital again, but this time he was declared unfit for active service. He was discharged in the summer of 1919 – "with a chip on my shoulder; a big heavy chip, probably some friend's thigh-bone".

J.B. suffered severely during the war but could never be certain of the extent its psychological effects had on him. But he did know he never lost his fear of travelling on the London Underground. In 1974 he used it as a setting for one of his few horror tales.

During the war, Priestley, who spent his twenty-first birthday in the trenches, encountered for the first time the rigid divisions of the English class structure, a system which had no place back home in Bradford. He hated its high-class snobs – and detested the callous, blundering generals and red-tabbed staff officers who represented them. "Mostly a lot of jackasses", he sneered. The few lads who had survived the slaughter agreed. "Lions led by donkeys" was how they described their dead mates.

J. B. Priestley, with false beard and holding a toy dog, tried out his histrionic gifts when he was a member of this concert party while convalescing after being wounded in the 1914–18 war. Hambleton Hall, August 1916.
(Source: Tom Priestley)

The lunacy of the top brass was superbly spotlighted half a century later by Sir Richard Attenborough in his film of *"Oh! What a Lovely War"* when, as a musical satire, one staff officer jumped right over another staff officer's back. "They were only playing leapfrog", mocked the singers. And, as Priestley discovered, they were.

Priestley came home to a devastated Bradford, his and its "time of innocence" long gone. The loss of the city's "brave boys" was enormous, especially the near wiping-out of the two Bradford Pals battalions during the Battle of the Somme. Out of 2,000 troops only 223 survived. There was hardly a Bradford street which had not lost someone.

Most of J.B.'s boyhood friends were dead – but not, praise be, his buddy Percy Monkman who, like Priestley, had survived the military horrors.

Considering his vast output, Priestley was to write little about the war – although he did write about it. This baffled those who thought such a massive human conflict would be ready grist to his literary mill.

In his memorable interview with J.B., John Braine asked him: "Why on earth haven't you used your war experience?" Priestley replied: "I'm not

J. B. Priestley in uniform, 1914.
(Source: Tom Priestley)

conscious of having deliberately avoided writing about the 1914 War. Probably during the earlier 'twenties I wanted to forget about it and anyhow I wasn't writing fiction then. Later, when I had had the necessary experience as a novelist, a number of very good books about the war had made their appearance, many of them saying just what I would have said. Incidentally, I wonder if you remember my account of the battalion reunion in 'English Journey'? If you don't know the book, you might take a look at that chapter sometime. You'll find your war there".

Priestley, I feel, wasn't giving the full reason for writing so rarely about the war. As well as depths of seriousness, he had a lively comic eye, and there was nothing comical

"Our P.O.W. Company football team. I am sitting on the major's left." 1919.
(Source: Tom Priestley)

about carnage. Not only this, the war had been a massive act of life-shrinking, spiritually as well as physically. As I emphasised earlier, Priestley had little time for activities which diminished the spirit of men.

Hardly had Priestley returned from the war before he was in full flow again as a writer. The *Yorkshire Observer* agreed to pay him a guinea a time for a series of articles on a walking trip he would make over the fells from Wharfedale to Wensleydale.

The *Yorkshire Observer*, which still came through the letter box of 5, Saltburn Place each morning, was a Bradford daily newspaper until the 1950s. It had a joint reporting staff with the evening *Telegraph & Argus*. I was a member of it for several years and my earlier interviews with J.B. appeared in the "Y.O." as we called it.

In *Delight* Priestley recalled: "I took with me into the Dales, like an enchanted passport, a commission from the editor of the 'Yorkshire Observer' to write several articles on my walking tour . . . It was my first commission of the kind . . . and I have never had one since that meant half as much".

Priestley wrote the articles under the pen-name Peter of Pomfret. I have been unable to discover why he chose the pseudonym, but he would have a motive. He did little without strong reason. Pomfret, of course, is another name for Pontefract which, with its blood-drenched castle, played a clamorous role during centuries of English history. Yet search as I did, I could find no Peter taking a prominent part in its story.

"I don't know really why he picked the pen-name", said Priestley's sister Winnie. "But I've a hunch he took it from something he had read".

Walking tour finished, Priestley said adieu to Bradford when through a Forces rehabilitation service he was given an educa-

Priestley with academic gown over officer's uniform.
(Source: Tom Priestley)

tional grant to study at Cambridge University. The grant was hardly adequate, so he supplemented his money by writing and lecturing.

Dorothy Fieldsend, that former Bradford teacher who hadn't been too impressed by J.B.'s piano skills, remembered his lecturing days. She commented: "The war was at last mercifully over with its million dead, though J.B. survived its horrors and was now studying at Cambridge. During the long vacation he came to our school to lecture to our senior girls on The Shakespearian Theatre. He brought with him a delightful, meticulously made model of the Globe Theatre complete in every detail, down to tiny metal balls to be rolled across the floor of the loft to imitate the sound of thunder.

"I remember being fascinated by this, as I have been so many times since by his extraordinary capacity for communicating to others his own enormous interest and detailed knowledge of people and places".

At Trinity College, Cambridge, the rebel in Priestley was astir again. The air of seeming superiority which emanated from the majority of those there, a lot of them from the upper classes, made him bridle – a not untypical reaction, even today, of Bradfordians to what they consider snootiness. While he had to eke out his small grant with a diet of mainly boiled eggs and bread and cheese, Priestley thought too many fellow students regarded the good things in life as their birthright. He felt too that they were contemptuous of his broad northern accent. He'd show 'em, though!

In 1921, J.B. won their applause by taking an impressive degree in history and political science, subjects he probably believed would complement and add weight to his already wide knowledge of literature.

More than half a century later, he was to confess with a typical self-jibe: "Cambridge society regarded me as a north-country lout of uncertain temper. And now fifty-five years too late, I realise that all those people were right".

Yet he was to tell me too: "Market Street and the Bradford of my youth taught me more about life than Cambridge ever did".

In the year of his winning university honours, Priestley was married, somewhat hurriedly, for the first time. Understandably many courtships were swift in those days. Young men who had been away at war had been starved of female companionship for far too long.

J.B.'s bride was Pat Tempest, the daughter of a Bradford neighbour. They had played piano and violin duets – and shared cuddles – in the back parlour of her home. Pat worked at Bradford's main public library, so her interest in literature wouldn't have been superficial.

At the time, John Braine's mother – tragically killed much later in a road accident at Thackley, Bradford, a loss from which John never fully recovered – also worked at the library. She date-stamped many a book for J.B.

With his Cambridge qualifications and a new wife to provide for, it would have been natural for Priestley to do as his father had done, make a career as a teacher or a lecturer.

But something nagged him, tormented him, beckoned him – and that something was the demand creativity was making. If we substitute the word "writing" for the word "music" the following extract from Priestley's *Johnson Over Jordan* was how J.B. must have felt at the time:

Priestley and his first wife, Bradford library assistant, Pat Tempest, 1924. (Source: Tom Priestley)

"The music doesn't belong to this place. But, then, neither do I. I lived in the world where that music was, but not for long. Never for long. It comes and goes so quickly. Just gleams and fades that other world like the light of sunset on distant hills. But perhaps that is real; that somewhere outside".

With considerable courage, Priestley, with less than fifty pounds, went in search of the somewhere outside – to London where he and Pat set up home in a flat at Waltham Green, a somewhat seedy district. For a period he augmented his income by working as a reader for a leading publishing house.

It must be understood that in those days opportunities for writers in London were much greater than they are now. The literary market was wide open, publications abounded, payments by comparison were much higher, and a large section of the population, knowing nothing of the snappy and attention-grabbing outpourings of television and the modern tabloid newspapers, were eager for expansive articles and informative books. During the years after the 1939–45 war the literary market quickly contracted, as a young John Braine, trying to make a writer's living in the capital, could have testified. He nearly starved.

Mrs Eli Tempest, Priestley's mother-in-law, with grandaughter Barbara. Summer 1924.
(Source: Tom Priestley)

Priestley had to work like a mad thing nevertheless to look after his family – for it soon was a family. His daughter Barbara was born in 1923 and daughter Sylvia a year later.

J.B. was good with children and altogether, in addition to his cherished step-daughter Angela, he had five, Mary, Rachel and his only son Tom being the others. The mother of the last named three was Priestley's second wife, Jane Wyndham Lewis.

It is not the purpose of this book to chart Priestley's life and career after his arrival in London. His connection and relationships with his home town is its chief concern.

Even so, it should be made clear that *The Good Companions*, published in 1929 and making Priestley a household name almost overnight, was not his first novel. By then he had not only written a book of verse, various miscellanies, five volumes of criticism and four books of essays, but two novels, *Adam In Moonshine* and *Benighted.*.

His efforts are all the more astonishing because in the mid-1920s his wife Pat developed cancer. Its ravages were quick and the struggle and misery awful.

Cruelly, it happened at the time his father was dying of cancer too. Priestley visited him in Bradford where they called at a pub and had a last glass of beer together. "He was easy in his mind about me at last; indeed pleased and proud", said J.B. "He did not know, because I never told him, that my wife, only in her middle twenties, was already going in and out of hospital with the cancer from which she died the following year; and that in the London where he thought I was doing well, I was half out of my mind with worry and overwork".

CHAPTER 10: PRETTY GIRLS WITH SAUCY CURLS

In the early 1970's I had a letter from J.B. which made clear he did have a romantic streak no matter how he might try gloss over it. The letter revealed how he still clung to the memory of a woman with whom he had fallen in love during his boyhood, had seen but once and never saw again.

Her name was Mabel Sealby and she had bewitched him when appearing in pantomime early this century at the Theatre Royal, Bradford.

Priestley asked if I could find out more about her. He said in his letter: "I have a very clear recollection of Mabel Sealby as principal girl in the Theatre Royal pantomime and I well remember she had a row with the management sometime about the middle of the run. Probably an old 'Who's Who In The Theatre' would give the date of her Bradford engagement".

I searched through those books and through many newspaper files, but regretfully didn't come across her name. It was not until after J.B. died that, thanks to Audrey Sykes, a collector of pictures of bygone theatre stars, I received a photograph of Miss Sealby, and an enchanting woman she looked.

Before sending me the photo, Audrey, one of the best ever amateur actresses at the Bradford Playhouse ("I would have had her in my company any time", retired actor-manager Sir Donald Wolfit once told me), had discovered the date of the Theatre Royal panto. The delectable Mable had played the title role in the 1905–6 Christmas–New Year production of Cinderella.

This was especially fascinating because it established that Priestley had fallen under the spell of Miss Sealby when he was eleven and not, as he thought, when he was fourteen. And don't let us fool ourselves. Children of eleven *can* fall in love – deeply.

Mabel Sealby as Cinderella, 1905–1906.
Priestley fell in love with Mabel Sealby when he was a boy.
(Photo courtesy of Peter Holdsworth)

71

In *Outcries and Aides* Priestley was to say: "I contrived to be in love with two different goddesses. One was Miss Mabel Sealby, who was playing principal girl in the Bradford Theatre Royal pantomime; the other, my own age, was the girl next door. As I wasn't allowed to do my own theatre-going then, I saw Miss Sealby only for one performance; I never wrote to her, never hung around the Stage Door. But her saucy black curls haunted me – she was not one of your altogether-too-demure principal girls, anaemic creatures – and every time she was mentioned in our local press then her name blazed out at me.

"When we were told she might be leaving the cast, after some saucy-curl dispute with the management, my city, dark enough, went into sable hangings", explained Priestley who, referring to the girl next door, said he was always seeing her – "but only through the side baywindow of our front room, where I loitered, just to catch a glimpse of her. The truth is, her parents and mine were not on friendly terms, and she and I never went to the same parties, so we never exchanged a word. Mine was simply a loitering-staring-dreaming relationship. Not a smile, not a look, rewarded me".

There are those who think (and I tend to go along with them) that Mabel Sealby was the inspiration behind one of Priestley's most captivating characters – Susie Dean, the concert party soubrette in *The Good Companions*. Like so many of his women characters, she is a delicious invention.

Even more delicious is Ruby Birtle, the perky, back-chatting maidservant in Alderman Helliwell's household in *When We Are Married*. J.B. told me that of all the characters he created, Ruby was his favourite – not his best because he considered the protagonists of his often hilarious satire, *The Image Men*, were that, but simply his favourite.

Spirited and pretty girls, especially with saucy curls, entranced Priestley in his youth – and how he enjoyed using those adjectives 'pretty' and 'saucy' when remembering them. They ranged from some of the lasses he chased during those Whitsuntide outings to the beauties he and his pals used to eye and follow during the open-air band concerts in Lister Park, Bradford.

In November 1964 J.B. made an absorbing speech at the open day of Belle Vue Boys' School's new premises. They were set in pleasant surroundings. During the speech he took up a remark of the chairman, Mr Frank Cooper, who had said that all the "good things" had been brought from the Manningham Lane school.

"That isn't true – they haven't brought the girls with them!", lamented Priestley. "I can tell you the last year I was there I was in love with no fewer than three of the girls. The air is pure. It is very fine here. But I think I would miss the girls".

When it came to attractive girls, Priestley was a normal, healthy and sometimes lusty youth; and if you read between many of his lines it is clear he had a deep, affectionate respect for them.

Girls of coarse nature could repulse him. Looking back to his Market Street days, he said: "If I left the office fairly early and it was a fine day, I would go along Manningham Lane as far as the park gates, then cut up Oak Lane. Sometimes I passed Lister's Mill just when all the girls and women were coming out, and they made me blush with loud bawdy calls that even today I prefer not to quote. Well away from Darley Street, Park Drive and the rest, and 'back o' t'mill' Bradford life could be rough and tough in those years".

In 1972 in *Over The Long High Wall* Priestley was forthright about his sexual attitudes. He made clear: "The writer you are reading now is an elderly heterosexual male, lusty indeed in his day and even now no envious fossil, who has enjoyed the physical relations of sexes, and with no objection to that, no shrinking from *this*, and without that feeling of guilt which seems to disturb some of my distinguished colleagues".

Nevertheless, he censured the over-emphasis on sex in modern society and declared: "Many people – men more than women, however – forget that the sexual act is a psychological as well as a physical experience and remains one, with a variety of consequences, on all levels. For good or ill, the psyche cannot be left out. The cool sensualist, the man-of-the-world type, who lumps together a good dinner, a bottle of wine, a cigar, and sex, whose roots go very deep, is deceiving himself".

Priestley had little time for men-of-the-world and was more comfortable in the company of women than he was at any get-together of macho males. He urged a larger place be found for fundamental feminine values.

Britain might benefit if the following Priestley statement was pinned to the walls of a million offices and factories:

> Our Western society, with America setting the pace, has clearly been increasingly dominated by the masculine principle. This can be discovered in its general aggressiveness, its desire to 'conquer' everything, its ruthless industrialism, its lack of concern for personal relationships and the state of our inner private world, its curious rootlessness and want of feeling for earth itself, its blind devotion to scientific and technological experiment at all costs. Now there may be plenty of individual women who accept and even admire this, but it is still safe to say that Woman herself, represented by the feminine principle, is deeply concerned with an entirely different set

of values. What I have listed above seems to her either idiotic or menacing. Existing in such a society, Woman has suffered a defeat and lives in an occupied country. She has been bribed to keep quiet by being given washing machines, racks of bright cheap dresses, more skinfoods and lotions. Our society may pet her but does not really share itself with her. So she feels discontented. (Yes, yes, yes, of course there are exceptions!) As if there had been some evil enchantment – *this is not her world.*

It is somewhat saddening that J.B. felt he had to make this statement because in June 1944, just a year before the second world war ended, he was much more optimistic. "Whether we like it or not we must look forward, not backward", he maintained when opening the Homes Of The Future exhibition in Leeds. "What kind of world is to come rests largely in the hands of our women. More than they imagine, they have the active means of influencing the world in which we must live. It is no use pretending that they do not know this. Women know that the structure of society depends upon the family unit; and with the vote they have the power of shaping what that structure should be".

Women had a staunch friend in Priestley, but this doesn't mean that his love for some of them did not cause emotional problems. He suffered all right – and so, in several instances, did they.

It is no secret that for a time he was in love with the magnificent actress Peggy Ashcroft ("She has the most beautiful voice I shall ever be allowed to hear", he said); and once there had been rumours that he was having an affair with Gracie Fields. His marriage to Jane Wyndham Lewis was a long but very uneasy one, with Priestley living frequently away almost like a bachelor.

Then, in 1953, he married the distinguished archaeologist and writer, Jacquetta Hawkes. She was a woman of fine mind, beauty and serenity and he loved her passionately.

"It took Jack a long, long time to find the right one", his sister Winnie commented. "But find her he did. He adored her and she adored him. In thanks, I should add that Jacquetta is and always has been very good to me".

Jacquetta Priestley, like Priestley's son Tom, was to prove a good friend to Bradford too.

CHAPTER 11: A HEAVY STONE OF GOLD

One of Priestley's great admirers is the actor and writer Leslie Sands. In his splendid book *Tuppence For The Rainbow*, an autobiographical account of his growing up in a working-class home in depression-hit Bradford, he recalls:

> One of our visits went as far afield as Morecambe, my grandmother's personal heaven-on-earth, where a new establishment was to be opened called The Sunshine Home for The Aged. Our little concert was to be the high-spot of the inaugural ceremony; and it was on our coach journey there that I learned from our ever-bubbling lady accompanist that the Home would be officially opened by Mr J. B. Priestley.
>
> I stood in the wings of the tiny stage and listened to his sympathetic and subtly humorous speech. He was thick-set and deep-voiced, had a face like crumpled brown paper that hid the most mischievous grins, and wore a navy-blue, chalk-stripe suit. But I hardly heard a word he said; for all the time I was listening with apparently rapt attention, I was thinking of *The Good Companions* and trying to realise that here, only a yard or so away from me, stood the man who had created them.
>
> He stayed on for our performance, and afterwards sat on an upturned barrel in the wings and talked to us about the theatre and the music-hall (of which he was always a staunch supporter). He had written *Dangerous Corner* by then and a couple of other successful plays into the bargain, as well as keeping up his regular output of the popular novel. It seemed to me, and the opinion has never altered, that here was a giant of our times, and a master of all the things that I was really interested in – the English language, the creation of books and plays, and their interpretation and dissemination. Oh, yes – I went home full of J. B. Priestley that night.
>
> 'Aye well', Grandma Sands said, when I gave her the customary and required account. 'He would be there, that chap. Allus likes to get his name in t'papers'.

It tickles me that "Allus likes to get his name in t'papers" because in Bradford then, and for a long time afterwards, liking to get your name in the newspapers was considered by many local people a crime only a few notches higher than attempting to murder your missus. It was scorned as a pinnacle of big-headedness, and, to put it mildly, Bradfordians didn't warm to big-heads.

As the 1920s advanced, Priestley, living away from Bradford, became more and more a target for disparagement. Yet he didn't seek publicity (he never did); the newspapers sought him. It was understandable. His reputation as an important writer was progressing with vast strides.

Percy Monkman's caricature of J. B. Priestley in *Bradford Civic Playhouse Personalities*, 1939. (Source: Peter Holdsworth)

But had he really turned his back on Bradford? No. During the decade, he returned to the city time and time again.

In 1922, for example, he made an appearance in opera in Bradford. Sir Thomas Beecham was launching the British National Opera Company at the Alhambra Theatre and, to strengthen the choruses of several presentations, a number of local people were enlisted. J.B. took the place of a friend and walked on in one of the productions.

"I wore tights with odd-coloured legs, and held an eight-foot pike outside a scenic church; I looked like a huge wasp", he recalled. "I got half-a-crown for one night and passed it on to the man whose place I had taken. Just for devilment, of course".

Not long afterwards he was back on native ground to give his first public lecture, urging the decentralisation of government, to an audience of "twenty or so damp and rather resentful citizens who had dragged themselves out" to listen to him on a rainy night in the West Riding.

During a later 1920s visit, Priestley didn't endear himself to some local folk when he criticised the red roofs of the dwellings on some Bradford

Priestley playing the tipsy "Yorkshire Argus" photographer during the first London run of *When We Are Married*. With him is the young Patricia Hayes as Ruby, the maidservant – J.B.'s favourite character.
(Source: Peter Holdsworth and *Telegraph & Argus*)

housing estates because, he insisted, "they do not melt into the background".

Perhaps J.B.'s most significant Bradford return during that period was in November 1927 when he addressed a large gathering of members of the Bradford English Society on the subject of his essays. He must have impressed because the following September he was elected president of the society, choosing "English Honour" for the title of his presidential address. Before the ceremony at the Technical College, he lunched with the Lord Mayor of Bradford, Alderman Michael Conway.

Soon afterwards, members of the Bradford English Society were privileged to become the first of the public to be introduced to what was to be one of Priestley's best loved characters – Jess Oakroyd who, in *The Good Companions*, tears up his insurance card, walks out of his unhappy Bruddersford home and eventually finds a welcome as the handyman with the Dinky Doos concert party. J.B. based Jess on an artisan friend of his father.

Priestley read to the members a part of the first chapter of what was to become a 250,000-word novel. It was published nine months later, in August 1929.

The Good Companions is huge in length and still huger in enjoyment. It swiftly and deservedly brought Priestley a rich return as well as international renown. Such was the stampede for copies that even in Bradford, where they had a fondness for bringing those artistically successful down a peg or two, the shops sold out almost immediately.

The book's instant triumph was more exceptional because the average novel of the day was of about 80,000 words. By making his novel so long, Priestley, almost in picaresque style, had returned to the practice of the great 19th century novelists.

Scott's novels, for example, averaged from 200,000 to 250,000 words, but he was comparatively brief. Dickens and Thackeray were much longer. *Martin Chuzzlewit* contains about 350,000 words and *David Copperfield* and *Bleak House* are even longer. Thackeray's *Newcomes* contains 450,000 words, and his shortest novel, *Esmond*, runs to 230,000.

George Eliot was almost as verbose in her *Middlemarch* and *Deronda*, and Dumas exceeded all English novelists in a matter of length.

The Good Companions had scarcely been published before a Bradford reviewer commented: "Anyone who is acquainted with Mr Priestley's previous books will anticipate that though the new one may be long it will never be tedious".

He was right – in the opinion of almost everyone but J.B. Priestley.

"I am sick to death of it!" he complained to me in his seventies. "I am fed up that so many people still seem to think I've written no other novel. It certainly isn't my favourite".

When the book came out, the nation went Good Companions crazy. Pairs of puppies on sentimental calendars were named The Good Companions; pictures of children holding hands were captioned The Good Companions; those displaying friendly relationships were tagged The Good Companions.

His book was not three years old when Priestley rebelled against the madness. He thundered:

Bradford actor Walter Williams as Alderman Helliwell in the history-making Bradford Playhouse production of *When We Are Married*. (Source: Peter Holdsworth)

"This is to give notice. On and after this date, if at any public dinner or meeting at which I am present I am referred to as 'a good companion', I shall forthwith leave the building. There is a limit and it has long ago been passed. For over two years I have suffered. I can recognise now, with sinking heart, a foolish gleam in the eyes of my fellow speakers, and I know it means that they are about to call me 'a good companion'. And they all say it as if it had never been said before, as if it was a sudden bold inspiration. Never was a man so pestered and haunted by the title of a book as I am. It begins to look as if I shall go down to the grave (and that at no far distant date) as a confounded good companion".

J.B. continued: "The book itself has sold about a quarter of a million copies in this country, and still goes on, and its title, which receives a hundred free advertisements every day, no doubt helped it. But nevertheless I wish I had called it something else. And let us get this straight, once and for all: The novel is not about some people who were good companions, but about some people who organised a concert party called The Good Companions. The people in question were not idyllically good-natured and self-sacrificing (except by

" WINNIE " PRIESTLEY— sister of the famous "J. B." —first and only secretary of the Civic Playhouse—did a great deal of preliminary spade- work (along with her late mother) when Playhouse was being formed—in addition to clerical duties devotes time and energy to promoting social activities—is equally at home serving coffee or selling pro- grammes as when entertaining distinguished visitors—has ful- filled practically all "offices" on both sides of footlights.

6

Winnie Priestley from Percy Monkman's series of caricatures in *Bradford Civic Playhouse Personalities*, 1939. (Source: Peter Holdsworth) comparison with some of the monsters that pass as characters now in fiction). They were an ordinary set of fairly decent mummers. Sometimes they were jealous of one another, let one down, bickered and quarrelled and got drunk, were silly and stupid. There was nothing astonishingly noble about them. But in an expansive moment – after supper – these people agreed to call their concert party The Good Companions. Hence the title of the book. Hence my misery. It would be just as sensible to keep referring to me as 'an angel' because a later (and, in my opinion, better) novel of mine is called *Angel Pavement*.

"There is nothing contemptible, I admit, in being known as a good companion (Though anybody who had been called it as many times as I have would be sick of it)", said Priestley. "There are many dubious things in life, but good companionship is obviously not one of them. But I have no claim to it. I am not one of those jovial hail-fellow-well-met men who are always to be found, the centre of a jolly group, in their club smoke rooms. I walk in and out of my club so gloomily that even now the servants are suspicious of my standing. I do not slap people on the back, and people do not slap me on the back – at least, not more than once".

If he thought an endeavour artistically worthwhile, Priestley was not one to turn down money, however. So it was that in November 1931 he was in his hometown to see a stage production of *The Good Companions* at the Bradford Alhambra.

He had seen the London version several times and he made clear that the Alhambra presentation was almost an exact replica of the West End show. "There is very little difference between them, and Bradford is fortunate in this respect: that the prices here are lower than at any other place on the tour".

Priestley was anxious to see for himself how Bruddersford (Bradford) took to Jess Oakroyd. He explained: "I noticed in Manchester, for instance, that certain lines spoken by Jess, which did not arouse particular interest in London, were received with enormous applause. I am more concerned about the show's reception in the North than in London where it has been a gigantic success. But if people here do not like it, I shall be really disappointed. If it were not a success in the North I should be more disappointed than if it had not been a success in London".

The Bradford staging *was* a success; and it was a smiling J.B. who, after the show, went to a party at the Connaught Rooms, Manningham Lane, which his stepmother gave to the members of *The Good Companions* company.

Over the years there have been many play productions of *The Good Companions* as well as a musical stage version starring Sir John Mills, two popular films and a more recent TV adaptation, much of it made at the Bradford Playhouse.

Yet Priestley was to feel that *The Good Companions* hung round his creative neck like a heavier and heavier stone. Even if it was a golden one!

CHAPTER 12: SAVING A THEATRE'S BACON

Early in 1929, the year *The Good Companions* was published, a meeting was held at the Priestleys' home in Saltburn Place. It proposed the formation of an enterprise which, unknown to those there, would revolutionise theatre in Bradford and eventually benefit considerably the performing arts throughout Britain. Had the meeting not taken place, many of today's prominent stage, film and television personalities might never have been given their early and essential opportunities.

Bradford is much in debt to those at the meeting. For they made possible the creation of the all-amateur Bradford Civic Theatre which, initially, was a co-operative offshoot of the then prestigious Leeds Civic Playhouse. The Playhouse in Leeds had been brought into being by Charles F. Smith who had a clothing factory in that city, and he readily gave Bradford's new baby encouragement and sterling assistance.

The Bradford Civic Theatre, officially inaugurated at a gathering at Church House, Bradford, in June 1929, soon attracted the participation of numerous members of the Bradford Playgoers' Society (J.B. had found its activities stimulating). It made its public debut three months later with an outstanding presentation of the medieval morality play, *Everyman*. This was performed on a stage constructed over the choir stalls in St. John's Church, Little Horton Lane.

Such was the triumph (it had an extended run) that it didn't take long before the Bradford Civic Theatre decided to go it alone. It set up home in the Jowett Hall in Chapel Street, Bradford (opposite the side entrance of Eastbrook Hall) which had previously been the headquarters of the Independent Labour Party. There, with money collections being taken during the intervals (the concern was originally a free admission theatre), quality production followed quality production, allowing Bradford to see many of drama's finest plays – plays it would otherwise have been denied. It was a policy which, with rare exceptions best forgotten, the organisation was to uphold and still upholds today – although it now has the title of the Bradford Playhouse and Film Theatre.

At the time of the Bradford Civic Theatre's inception, liaison between Leeds and Bradford was undertaken by Ronald Giffen who deserves top credit for spearheading the project. He was later to stage manage some of the London productions of Priestley's plays.

Robert Giffen was a valued friend of J.B.'s stepmother Amy, herself a keen theatregoer. As well as having its professional theatres, Bradford in those days boasted a profusion of amateur stage societies and Amy supported many of them. "She loved going anywhere to see a play, even when father didn't accompany her", said her daughter Winnie. "I remember he once flatly refused to go with her when a Greek company came to the Theatre Royal. That didn't stop her, though. She came back fascinated, even if she had been a bit baffled by it all".

Number 5 Saltburn Place seemed an ideal choice therefore for that first pioneering meeting.

Unlike some people think, J.B. was *not* at the meeting; he was busy in London at the time. But Amy was. And so was Winnie. They were both to serve the new venture with distinction – Amy as a member of the management committee and Winnie as its first and very hard-working secretary, a position she held for numerous years.

J.B. was elected president of the new organisation and he held the office for 25 years. He was more than a figure-head; he increasingly contributed to its activities.

Winnie chuckled: "Jack was no fool, and he was quick to realise that the 'Civic', as we called it then, might prove an ideal platform for some of his works as well as being a place where he could try-out plays while amending and polishing them if he thought that necessary".

The Bradford Civic Theatre soon flourished, with its director James R. Gregson (himself no mean hand as a playwright) and scenic artist Philip Robinson giving some dynamic leadership.

Then, early in 1935, disaster seemingly struck. The Jowett Hall was destroyed by fire. But members refused to be beaten. The setback only spurred them to keener endeavours. Under their then chairman, the late Thomas Boyce, Bradford's Director of Education, they set about raising funds to build a new showpiece little theatre to be designed by architect Eric Morley and to stand on the site of the Jowett Hall.

The 'Civic's' specially formed Travelling Theatre, which toured productions by lorry, sometimes to far distant Dales villages, helped boost enormously scores of fund-raising efforts. One of these was a production of Priestley's bitter-sweet comedy, *Cornelius*, which J.B., a pillar subscriber, "donated" with his blessings. Not only this, he spent several nights advising the cast.

The clouds really lifted for the fund-raisers when the late Tom Padgett, a prominent local builder, guaranteed what in those days was the enormous sum of £5,000. This enabled the 299-seat new theatre to become a reality in record time. It chose for its title the Bradford Civic Playhouse.

It was opened by Sir Barry Jackson in 1936 and its first presentation was the world premiere of Priestley's *Bees On The Boatdeck* which, although a comedy, took note of the kind of Nazi fervour which would soon throw nations into turmoil. It was directed by James R. Gregson. Memorable in the cast were Nell Ackroyd (later she became Mrs. Bill Walker) and Edward Thornton who took the lead.

Among the audience were Sir Cedric Hardwick and Miss (not yet Dame) Edith Evans who was to become a Playhouse honorary vice-president. She was so impressed by the standards of the performances and the production she had seen that she inquired incredulously: "Do you mean to tell me that you do it *all* in your spare time?"

Edward Thornton, a successful Bradford woolman who had worked his way up from humble beginnings, was an unusual man. He was led into the ways of meditation during the 1939–45 war, and after it studied for four years under Jung. He wrote a book called *The Diary of a Mystic* and I reviewed it in the *Telegraph & Argus*.

Later I received a letter from his London address and in it he explained that, although the book had won attention from both abroad and in this country, the Bradford review "touched me more". He explained: "I feel, in a very small way, something of what C. G. Jung expressed when his

Bradford Arts Club Supper, 1938. Priestley seated in centre.
(Source: Bradford Libraries)

old university of Basel finally honoured him towards the end of his life. He had been honoured by almost every major seat of learning in the world, but when *'his own people'* remembered him, his emotion was very touching to witness'.

I include the extract because you could relate it to the way the inner Priestley felt. Years ago Winnie said to me: "Jack would never admit it, but I know him. The only honour he wants deep down is, I'm certain, for Bradford to honour him".

Priestley wasn't much impressed by honours of other kinds. He turned down a knighthood, a life peerage and the opportunity to become a Companion of Honour.

The Priestley creation which will always be associated with the Bradford Playhouse is *When We Are Married*. It is not only one of the funniest half-dozen English comedies so far written, but underneath it is, like Oscar Wilde's *The Importance of Being Earnest*, a superb social satire. Again like *The Importance of Being Earnest*, you could not delete a line, never heed a passage, without injuring it. As a marvel of character and play construction, it is perfect. It is miraculous that J.B. should have written it during the 1938–39 two-year period when he gave the public two new novels, an autobiography and two other plays, one of them being the marvellous *Johnson Over Jordan*. "I felt like making myself laugh for a change", he grinned when I asked what prompted him to write it.

When We Are Married was to be staged many times at the Bradford "Civic" and more than once it was to save the Playhouse's financial bacon. People flocked to see it.

In Chapel Street in 1938 it made theatre history because, thanks to J.B.'s persuasion, permission was given for the Playhouse to present the amateur premiere of *When We Are Married* at the same time as the play's opening run at St. Martin's Theatre, London – an unheard of kindness.

Walter Williams, a notable Bradford actor and producer (and later a drama festival adjudicator), who played Alderman Helliwell in the amateur premiere, was, many years later, to tell Liz Ambler of BBC Radio Leeds: "The first week we played *When We Are Married* we had to turn some people away. It was a terrific success. We wrote to London and said 'Please may we do it another week?', and London very nicely said yes. So we played it a second week. By this time the queues grew. They were down to the bottom of Chapel Street. So then we asked for a third week. By this time the queues were down Chapel Street and up Leeds Road. So we asked for a fourth week. And London said, 'Not on your life! Not on your nelly! Come off it! We've got to run this thing here. But they did promise us – a promise which was honoured by the way – that when it was released for amateurs we should have the option to do it first. And about eighteen months later we played it for a fortnight".

During the same radio programme, J.B.'s friend Percy Monkman, who portrayed Herbert Soppitt in the amateur premiere, recalled: "I think the Playhouse owes a great debt to *When We Are Married*. It saved the theatre financially because you could guarantee a packed house every time – at every performance".

When We Are Married takes place in the sitting room of Alderman Helliwell's house in Clecklewyke, an imaginary West Riding town, not long before the 1914–18 war. Three successful couples, full of self-esteem and all "big at t'chapel", get together for a joint silver wedding celebration when they learn, like a bombshell dropped, that they might not have been married officially at all. It appears they could have been living in sin for a quarter of a century. Not surprising, consternation and pandemonium break out.

Percy Monkman, by day a chief cashier with a bank, reflected: "There were quite a few occasions when the current Lord Mayor, with his entourage, came to see *When We Are Married* and said of this or that character, 'Isn't that like so-and-so' – when it was probably just like them".

There were critics who would claim that all the characters in *When We Are Married* were nothing but caricatures. Percy's observation confirms that is not so. They had backbones of reality; and Priestley's eye for West Riding social behaviour and niceties, of a kind which was to exist until after the second world war, never mind the first, was superbly perceptive.

I can vouch that Henry Ormonroyd, the squiffy "Yorkshire Argus" photographer in the play, was no exaggeration. In my teens I worked alongside quite a few old soaks, including one who in spirit (or should it be spirits?) could have been Henry's fellow soul. Talented he was. Responsible he definitely wasn't. And he was a reporter, not a photographer. Like Ormonroyd, he managed to get himself fired.

I remember his telling me that he had been "having a jolly good time" at the home of a certain lady friend when he noticed that on the wall over the bed was a text proclaiming "God is the unseen witness in this house". "So I quickly turned it the other way", he laughed. Henry Ormonroyd would have patted him on the back.

Because his father had been stage-manager at the Bradford Empire, he wrote an article about that music hall, incorporating theatrical stories his dad had told him. Priestley read it and passed on his gratitude.

The *When We Are Married* scenes between Ormonroyd and Ruby, the cheeky maid, are perhaps the funniest of the play. The following extract is, I suggest, a classic example of how to write a comic stage encounter:

(Ruby ushers in Ormonroyd, who is carrying his camera, etc., and is now very ripe.)

ORMONROYD (advances into the room and looks about him with great care, then returns to Ruby.) Nobody here. (He gives another glance to make sure.) Nobody at all.

RUBY (up L.C.). They'll all be back again soon. They're mostly in the dining-room – fratchin'.

ORMONROYD (C.). What – on a festive occasion like this?

RUBY. That's right.

ORMONROYD. Well, it just shows you what human nature is. (He wanders to R.C.) Human nature! T-t-t-t-t. I'll bet if it had been a funeral – they'd have all been in here, laughing their heads off. (He looks closely at the cigars on the table R.C.). There isn't such a thing as a cigar here, is there?

RUBY (moving down C.). Yes, yer looking at 'em. D'you want one? 'Ere. (As he lights it.) Me mother says if God had intended men to smoke He'd have put chimneys in their heads.

ORMONROYD (comes to her R.). Tell your mother from me that if God had intended men to wear collars He'd have put collar-studs at back of their necks. (He stares at her.). What are you bobbing up an' down like that for?

RUBY. I'm not bobbing up an' down. It's you. (She laughs and regards him critically.) You're a bit tiddly, aren't you?

ORMONROYD (horror-struck). Tidd-ldly?

RUBY. Yes. Squiffy.

ORMONROYD (surveying her mistily). What an ex't'rornry idea! You seem to me a mos' ex't'rornry sort of – little – well, I dunno, really – what's your name?

RUBY. Ruby Birtle.

ORMONROYD (tasting it). Umm – Ruby –

RUBY. All right, I know it's a silly daft name, you can't tell me nowt about Ruby I 'even't been told already – so don't try.

ORMONROYD (solemnly). Ruby, I think you're quite ex't'rornry. How old are you?

RUBY (quickly). Fifteen – how old are you?

ORMONROYD (waving a hand, vaguely). Thousands of years, thousands and thousands of years. (He turns away R.)

RUBY (coolly). You look to me about seventy.

ORMONROYD (turns back, horrified). *SEVENTY!* I'm fifty-four.

RUBY (severely). Then you've been neglectin' yourself. (Ormonroyd looks at her, breathing hard and noisily.) Too much liftin' o' t'elbow.

ORMONROYD (after indignant pause). Do you ever read the "Police News"?

RUBY. Yes. I like it. All 'orrible murders.
ORMONROYD. Then you must have seen them pictures of women who've been chopped up by their husbands –
RUBY (with gusto). Yes – with bloody 'atchets.
ORMONROYD (impressively). Well, if you don't look out, Ruby, you'll grow up to be one of them women.

The scene is sheer comic bliss. So it seemed only right that Priestley, who was generously to allow the Bradford Playhouse to perform in perpetuity *When We Are Married* without paying royalties, should himself be given the opportunity to play photographer Henry. He did so for several nights at St. Martin's Theatre, London, when Frank Pettingell (perhaps the best of all Ormonroyds) was unable to appear. The St. Martin's production caused widespread attention too when, in November 1938, it became the first play ever to be televised from a theatre stage.

After the amateur premiere of *When We Are Married*, Priestley, who thought that, generally, West Riding non-professionals were better at performing the play than 'pros' – "It fits them like a glove", he said), was to visit and be associated with the Bradford Playhouse many more times; and it must have cheered him when it became acknowledged in many parts of the world (if seldom in Bradford) as one of Europe's best non-professional theatres.

During the second world war, Esme Church, of Old Vic fame, produced such impressive productions for the Playhouse that she was asked to become Playhouse director. Not only did she agree, but under the aegis of the Playhouse inaugurated and ran the nearby Northern Theatre School where so many now outstanding actors and producers are trained. Many of them appeared in Playhouse productions.

Among the distinguished who were to learn their craft at the Playhouse or at the Theatre School (or both) were producers William Gaskill, James Hill, David Giles and Peter Dews; actresses Billie Whitelaw, Polly Hemingway, Thelma Barlow, Ruth Mitchell and Mary Tamm; actors Robert Stephens, Bernard Hepton, Edward Petherbridge, Gorden Kaye, Peter Firth, George Layton, Dudley Foster, William Lucas, Arnold Yarrow, George Little, David Roper, Tom Bell, Philip Stone, Duncan Preston and Bruce Bould; and playwright Donald Howarth.

One prominent name must be added to this list. It is that of the late Tony Richardson who, after experience at the Playhouse and with Shipley Young Theatre, went on to become famous in theatre and films. In May 1956 his name was on the Bradford Alhambra playbills as the director of a memorable production of *The Scandalous Affair of Mr. Kettle and Mrs. Moon*. Its author was J. B. Priestley.

CHAPTER 13: HE CAME TO A CITY

During the 1930s and 40s, when not a few local people were complaining, "Oh, him! He's turned 'is back on us", Priestley was in Bradford frequently. The author, who in 1943 would have his play *They Came to a City* premiered in Bradford, ought to have had a tribute written about *him*. It should have been called "He Came to a City".

J.B. must have been saddened, therefore, by the undercurrents of belittlement which ferociously, if temporarily, broke surface after the 1934 publication of his *English Journey*, a masterpiece of travel and social criticism. A local alderman offered in print to fight him if he ever came near his beloved city again.

"I wondered at the time", remarked J.B., "if he imagined I was a weedy, spectacled scribbler. Perhaps I should have put it on record that I weighed fourteen stones and still took a certain amount of violent exercise".

Priestley wasn't a man to check his rebel spirit, no matter how civic luminaries might rage. Of *English Journey* he explained: "In that book I tried to set down honestly my impressions of the various industrial districts I visited, and so found myself compelled to say that many of them were extremely ugly or dreary or depressing. No sooner was it out than a cataract of protest and abuse descended on me".

A few Bradfordians were in the vanguard of those trying to drown his voice.

The 1930s had started quite amicably with J.B. opening the annual exhibition of works by members of the Bradford Arts Club of which his friend Percy (nearly always wearing a bow tie) was a leading light.

In May 1932, Priestley was again in Bradford and was invited to open the extensions to the Bradford Central Library in Darley Street. He was back a year later – this time to gather material for his *English Journey* – when the Arts Club honoured him with a well attended dinner.

Even when the *English Journey* storm broke, Priestley displayed to north country denigrators that, whatever they might think, his affection for the West Riding still ran deep. Although never a dialect writer professionally, he contributed from his home in the south this choice piece to John Hartley's Clock Almanack:

> Ah remember t'owd 'Clock Almanack' when Ah wur a little lad, an' Ah hope it'll still be on t'goa when Ah'm an owd man, if 'ivver Ah get to be an owd man. (An', sitha, Ah'm noan so sure abaht that.) Ah'll tell yer for

why. 'Clock Almanack's a gooid owd West Riding institution. An' it keeps t'dialect i' print. Ah wish some o' these fowk ahtside Yorkshire would tak' a gooid look at it, one o' these days, an' then we wouldn't get these Sahth Country clever heads makkin' Yorkshiremen say, 'By gum, Ah'm oop for t'coop'. They do tell me dahn here (though Ah doan't tak much notice, for they knaw nowt) that t'wool trade's on t'mend. Ah'd like to see t'Almanack have t'biggest year it ivver had. Onny how, Ah mun have a copy me-sen. It'll keep me i' toit for a bit.

Priestley, who would you believe was once seriously written about in a national newspaper as J.B. (Ba gum) Priestley, was to "keep i' toit' with Bradford for far more than a bit. For example, as well as *Bees On The Boatdeck* he allowed the Bradford Civic Playhouse to present premieres of *I'm a Stranger Here* which was later renamed *People at Sea* (1937), *I Have Been Here Before* (1938) and *Bull Market* (1943).

Although the world premiere of *I'm a Stranger Here* took place only a few days before J.B. was due to leave for a lecture tour in America, he worked eighteen hours a day helping to shape the production at the little theatre which had come to mean so much to him.

During this period, Priestley's Clock Almanack item had become so appreciated that the Yorkshire Dialect Society made him a vice-president. He had already become a member.

May 1941 saw Priestley in Bradford to open the Margaret McMillan Nursery Centre at Friendship House, Greaves Street. He was a great admirer of McMillan and her pioneering work and he praised the city for once more being at the forefront in the struggle for better social conditions. That evening he was given a reception at the Cartwright Memorial Hall.

Later in 1941 J.B. was at the Prince's Theatre, Bradford, to see a presentation of his new play, *Goodnight Children*. He took the opportunity of getting some local colour for a Boxing Day broadcast, *The Return of Mr. Oakroyd*.

Priestley received national attention in January 1943 when he world premiered *They Came to a City* at the Bradford Prince's. Its subject was on the minds of millions at the time – namely the problem of reconstruction after the war.

Priestley told Bradford journalists that the London management with which he was then associated had never considered Bradford a place to be visited in the early stages of a play, but he and the cast of *They Came to a City* intended to prove the management wrong. They did.

Book display by Wilson's of Kirkgate, 1930.
(Source: Tom Priestley)

Bradford again offered the contradiction that, although many of its people continued to snipe at Priestley, its citizens (during this period anyway) still rushed to see and applaud his plays.

They Came to a City had some excellent actors and actresses. They included John Clements, Googie Withers, A. E. Matthews, Raymond Huntley and Ada Reeve. They were all given a civic welcome.

During the play's Bradford run, J.B. presented a self-portrait of the Bradford-born painter, Richard Eurich, to the Cartwright Hall for inclusion in the permanent collection.

Soon afterwards Bradford had another visit from Priestley when he attended a private preview of the film of *They Came to a City* at the Bradford Playhouse where in 1945 he opened a two-week summer drama school. The same year he opened the new headquarters of the Bradford branch of the Society for Cultural Relations with the U.S.S.R. in Laycock's Rooms where many organisations held meetings. J.B. had attended some of them in his youth.

"I happen to have been in Russia", Priestley was to say three years later, adding: "I am not a Communist. I am not even a 'fellow traveller'. But the most sincere statements I have heard about war and peace I heard from ordinary men and women in Russia".

In 1947 J.B. wanted to present another premiere – *The Linden Tree* – at the Bradford Prince's, but owing to a misunderstanding and some rancour between his production manager and the theatre management about the booking of the theatre, his wish was not fulfilled. However, a year later, Francis Laidler, whose theatre the Prince's was, telephoned Priestley to offer the building for his next play. So in October 1948 Bradford saw the premiere of *Home Is Tomorrow*.

Sentiment apart, why did J.B. decide that Bradford audiences should see so many of his plays before the rest of the country? "They're wonderful audiences", he commented at the time. "They want their money's worth, and they want something to chew over".

Although *Home Is Tomorrow* had a cheering reception at the Prince's, London didn't take to it. It closed there after a month – even though its cast included such splendid performers as Leslie Banks, Irene Worth, Cecil Trouncer and Alan Wheatley.

Priestley considered *Home Is Tomorrow* a fine play. It is set in the Caribbean and centres on a civil servant who not only supports the United Nations Underdeveloped Territories Organisation, but finds on the island in his charge that he likes "ordinary, messy, blundering people".

When in Bradford, Priestley said of the play: "It presents all the problems we are arguing about today. It is not the dramatist's job to offer solutions to problems. What he offers is a certain kind of experience – a dramatic experience and an emotional experience, and let the audience use their imagination to solve the problem for themselves. Mind you, as a private individual I'll solve your problems right, left and centre".

This is an important statement because it underscored Priestley's habit of playing a favourite trick on audiences – and that was to present them with ideas which initially appeared ordinary but turned out to be anything but. He could not have done this if he had over-poetically slanted his dialogue, something unappreciated by the reviewers who complained there was no poetry in him.

Before the 1940s were out, there was to be another Priestley premiere at the Prince's. This was of *Summer Day's Dream* in August 1949. It looked into the future and invited audiences to face up to what might occur if England was devastated by an atomic war. In the cast were Herbert Lomas, Czech actress Adina Mandlova, Eileen Thorndike, John Westbrook and a young Adrienne Corri. As usual Bradford gave the play a loud ovation.

An item of interest: Among the character actors in the professional production of Priestley's *I Have Been Here Before* was the Bradford-born actor Wilfrid Lawson who will be remembered by many of J.B.'s juniors as Joe Lampton's gravel-voiced uncle in the film *Room at the Top*. An old boy of Hanson School, he was notorious for getting drunk. I once bumped into him as he staggered out of the Midland Hotel, Bradford.

Yet he could be an electrifying performer on stage or screen. Priestley was to say of him: "He could be a hell of a nuisance, especially if you were part of his management, but Wilfrid Lawson was indeed a remarkable actor, a kind of diminished and later version of Edmund Kean, with beer instead of brandy".

CHAPTER 14: THAT STEAMING PIE

Beginning at 10.30 p.m. on August 31st, 1940, Bradford had its biggest air raid of the second world war. It was watched by Priestley's sister Winnie from the window of her attic room at 5, Saltburn Place – the room which had once been her brother's.

"You could look down on the city centre, and the highest flames, I learned next day, came from the badly hit Lingard's store", she recalled.

Priestley was swift in coming to see the damage for himself. It greatly upset him, although he was no stranger to the terrors from the sky. For example, in London, during one week alone, he lived through three nights of personal danger.

The experience began when he booked a bedroom in an hotel adjacent to Broadcasting House so that it would be handier to carry out some early hours broadcasts to the United States.

One night he decided to go to bed early when he was told a special broadcast in America had been arranged at the last moment. He stayed out of bed and went to Broadcasting House instead. While he was there a bomb fell through the hotel, close to the bedroom in which he would have been sleeping.

It did not do much damage to his room, but it made it impossible for him to recover his personal belongings immediately.

Next evening he went again to Broadcasting House. That night a second bomb fell through the hotel. This time it destroyed his bedroom and everything he had there. On the third night a friend offered a bed in a basement shelter in his house. J.B. readily accepted the hospitality, and went to bed feeling secure. But no! He was asked to get up and get out quickly. An incendiary bomb had fallen on the house and it was on fire.

Priestley's visit to bomb damaged Bradford inspired what was to become his most famous (if not, in his opinion, best) Sunday night *Postscript* talk to the nation, the one mentioning Roberts' pie shop in Godwin Street.

He said: "It was far more of a shock to me to see a few burnt-out buildings in Bradford than all the damage in London. It was astonishing to discover the familiar large drapery store and the old chapel no longer there, and to see other places broken ruins and odd pillars and bits of wall still standing. They had an unexpectedly dignified look – rather picturesque ruins with a hint of Pompeii or the Herculaneum about them. I think the sight made a far deeper impression on me than the bombing I had seen in London. It brought together two entirely different worlds – the safe and shining world of my childhood and this lunatic world of today. I was appalled by the sheer stupidity of it. These Nazi airmen had flown hundreds of miles to destroy an old chapel, a few stores, and damage a cinema. Nothing that will make the least difference to our war efforts, nothing that cannot be replaced except the old walls of the chapel".

Priestley mentioned that Lingard's store was starting up again, and he went on to describe how the pie shop he knew so well as a schoolboy was still in business, although damaged in the raid.

He went on: "Ever since I can remember, there has been behind this drapery store a small eating house specialising in meat and potato pie, one of those little Dickensian places which still survive in provincial towns. I remember it well because there had always been a giant, almost superhuman meat and potato pie in the window with a magnificent brown, crisp, wrinkled, succulent-looking crust. Not only that, but out of that pie came rich puffs of steam which made the mouth water. It was a perpetual volcano; that steaming brown pie was, to my boyish mind, as much an essential part of my native city as the Town Hall and its chimes".

Priestley said that having heard the famous pie had been destroyed in the raid, he went to see for himself; but there it was steaming away as ever, "every puff of steam defying Hitler and Goering and the whole gang of them".

"I asked the owner what had happened and he answered shortly after that the shop had had its front blown out but was now open, and the pie had not been damaged at all, because it was his habit always to remove it to a place of safety each night".

Priestley said he was conscious of being politely ushered from the doorway. "I think they thought I was doing a little fifth column work to discover the secret of the steaming pie. But a little later the pieman came up to me and greeted me heartily. It seems that his wife, who was in the shop, had recognised my voice".

It was then that the pieman told J.B. something he yearned to know as a boy and had often wondered about since – how the perpetual puffs of steam had been produced from the pie for the past forty or fifty years. Priestley was never to reveal the secret.

The pie shop, which as time passed was to display a notice proclaiming "J. B. Priestley paid us a visit, why don't you?", closed in June 1955 when its owner, Mrs Roberts, retired. Before his death eleven years before, she had promised her husband that she would neither sell the business as a pie shop nor pass on its name.

When he heard about Mrs Roberts' retirement, Priestley reminisced: "I was looking for a topic for my Sunday night Postscript, happened to see the steaming great pie, and turned it rather hastily into a sort of humorous symbol of Britain's endurance.

"To my astonishment, this little talk instantly became one of my most popular Postscripts. I was surprised because I did not think then – and do not think now – that it was actually one of the best of these talks. But the listeners were not of this opinion.

"There was a double irony in the wild success of this talk on the pie. Very soon I was bored by all the complimentary references to it. Then later I began to feel irritated and annoyed. For years strangers would come up to me, not to talk about my books and plays but about this pie Postscript. However much we may enjoy praise, it is all too easy to feel irritation when the results of years of solid work are ignored and at the same time far too much attention is focused on a mere trifle. More than once I wished I had never mentioned the pie.

"The further irony was that the owner of the shop shared this wish. He had all the business he wanted, had a refreshing contempt for mere publicity, and was genuinely annoyed by all the fuss that immediately followed the broadcast. Let me add here that this attitude delighted me. I was entirely on his side.

"The fame suddenly thrust upon him and his shop seemed to him just a confounded nuisance. People came for miles to stare at his window. Already, you may say, the permanent silly season of this post-war age, was beginning to shape itself. And the pie owner wanted none of it. And I said then, "Good luck to him".

"Nevertheless, if the pie, the steaming window, the old eating place itself, will soon vanish for ever, then I am genuinely sorry. But not because there was once a Sunday night in the war when millions heard about the pie and talked about it for some days.

"No, I regret its disappearance because, like its owner, it had character. I have not been told what will take the place of that old steaming window, but I shall be surprised if it is anything I would think worth writing about, even for the purpose of doing a ten-minute broadcast.

"I do not suggest that the pie should be kept, still steaming away in the Cartwright Hall, the Central Library, or the Town Hall. I do not see it as a museum object, which might turn up one night on 'Animal, Mineral or Vegetable?' to be spotted at once by my friend – and, in youth, a fellow Bradfordian – Sir Mortimer Wheeler. Let it steam, especially when we are feeling peckish, in our memories".

Hundreds of Bradfordians (myself among them) remember Roberts' pie shop with relish. One of them with particular vivid memories was a pupil at Bradford Grammar School when, to help his father, he often delivered chests of tea to the pie shop. "There were scores of pint pots there, so customers must have drunk an enormous amount," he says. "I used to take the chests into the cellar where there was peggy tub after peggy tub of potatoes. Under modern disciplines, they would have had to call the dish they sold potato and meat pie", he laughed.

The name of the lad was Ken Morrison and he is now the multi-millionaire chairman and managing director of William Morrison Supermarkets.

And the secret of the steaming pie?

It was quite simple, and was eventually revealed after Mrs Roberts' retirement. All it involved was a tube fixed to the bottom of the imitation pie, a tube which was attached to a steaming kettle in the cellar.

15.   BLACK DAYS FOR THE WHITE COUNTESS

Although crime has increased and common courtesy declined, Bradford generally is a far more compassionate and tolerant city than it was forty years ago when it was still influenced by the Victorian puritanism and prudery which had once made Bradford a Nonconformist stronghold. It can't be easy for those not old enough to remember the early 1950s to appreciate how harsh some Bradfordians could be when judging others. But they were harsh – as J. B. Priestley was to discover.

The decade had started well enough. In 1951, Festival of Britain year, Priestley embarked on something of a one-man crusade for a festive Britain, castigating the people who grumbled that the time was inappropriate for such jollifications in his novel *Festival at Farbridge*. He pressed home his campaign on the people of the West Riding when he opened a Festival exhibition of works by Bradford artists at Cartwright Hall.

He declared that if any people really deserved to hold such a celebration, the English did, and he expressed dismay and disappointment at the West Riding contribution which, he considered, did not truly represent the glory and grandeur of that part of the world.

Artist Richard Eurich presented a pipe to Priestley who observed, amid a roar of laughter, that he knew he would get something if only he came to Bradford often enough!

One year later it was a different story. Bradford gave him nothing – except a rebuff – when he asked to be allowed to present *Dragon's Mouth* there on a Sunday evening. J.B., whose marriage to Jane Wyndham Lewis was dissolved in 1952, had written this work in collaboration with Jacquetta Hawkes, wife of Professor Christopher Hawkes. It broke new ground for Priestley, being a dramatic reading, not a play. It had a quartet of characters, but was not costumed. The four taking part wore evening dress and carried scripts. There was neither stage lighting nor scenery.

Even so, Bradford wasn't having it. Sunday night entertainment rules were Sunday night entertainment rules, it insisted. How Priestley, who rebelled against those Sunday evenings of his youth, must have despaired when the Bradford Fire Services Committee refused him permission to present *Dragon's Mouth*. "I might have been asking for a licence to sell bootlaces on the Town Hall steps", he exclaimed.

The refusal was as nothing compared with what happened in 1953. For in the June of that year the fat was really in the Bradford fire for Priestley when he was cited as co-respondent in an undefended divorce suit brought by Professor Hawkes.

J.B. recalled: "In the early 1950s I figured in a divorce case, though I was not called upon to give evidence, and was not represented in court. This did not prevent the judge, notorious in legal circles for his love of publicity, from telling the world my conduct had been 'mean and contemptible', a conclusion based on slender evidence that he did not even understand. A large section of the English Press, almost gleefully, splashed this 'mean and contemptible' across its pages, doing the dirty on me in millions of homes. Now, looking back on my life, I realise that on innumerable occasions I must have behaved badly – being inconsiderate, bumptious, over-bearing, stupidly insensitive, as if determined to remain an adolescent lout. I plead guilty to a score of faults. Even so, after searching hard, I cannot recall an occasion when my conduct was mean and contemptible, nor do I remember anybody ever charging me with such conduct – until of course this judge had to speak his piece and fifty editors rushed his slander into print. And equally of course I had to grin and bear it, having no means of redress".

Priestley's self-chastisement (over-the-top as it was) is fascinating because he was never an adolescent lout; and his mention of being bumptious, over-bearing and stupidly insensitive could have described more justly not a few Bradfordians who were his contemporaries.

The general Bradford reaction to the divorce was cruel and deplorable. I can vividly remember comments, even in my own street, which were savage in their censure. Nor will I forget overhearing, while walking along a Town Hall corridor, one city father saying to another: "No longer want to know t'chap; no longer want him here!"

It was all shameful.

Jack and Jacquetta, who were married at Caxton Hall in July 1953, were so obviously in love – and were to remain so – that had most of today's younger Bradfordians been able to attend the ceremony they would have showered the couple with good wishes.

Priestley braved out the slander, though. So much so that, in March 1954, he was back in Bradford for the English premiere of *The White Countess* at the Prince's Theatre – thanks to the encouragement of an understanding management. During the 1950s, in my view, theatre people were in the main far more tolerant than the public of others' personal relationships.

For Jack and Jacquetta Priestley *The White Countess* proved an unhappy endeavour. They had written it together and J.B. would not have been human if did not feel protective towards his new wife.

The play centred on an Austrian noblewoman in the Napoleonic era who, loved by four men and bored with her unfree life and her husband, sought fulfilment as a woman. It got a panning.

Critic Bob Staton wrote in the *Telegraph & Argus*: "There is something very saddening in the sight of a great author and playwright floundering as Mr. J. B. Priestley does in *The White Countess*. Michael Colbert, who mistakenly thought the work 'another Time play', observed in the *Yorkshire Observer*: "The play lumbers along like a gun carriage". And Barrie Heads wrote in *The Yorkshire Post*: "The authors say of *The White Countess* that it is 'a romantic comedy of ideas'. The authors are J. B. Priestley and his wife, Jacquetta Hawkes, and their statement of intentions is welcome, for it makes their aim clearer than anything in the play".

The White Countess, which starred the superb actor Robert Harris (he won acclaim even if the play didn't) and Hollywood's Swedish star Viveca Linfors (the Priestleys had been much impressed when they saw her in a John van Druten play in New York), was presented by impresario Lord Vivian who had been a partner of the grand old showman C. B. Cochran.

A fortnight before its English premiere in Bradford, the play had a try-out in Dublin. The *Yorkshire Observer*'s man in Ireland went to see it and reported back that *The White Countess* "is the most disappointing play Priestley has ever written". His criticism was given prominence in the paper – a decision which annoyed Priestley.

On the day after the play's Bradford first night I was on my way to the office when, from far across the road, I spotted J.B. and his wife as they walked from the Prince's down Little Horton Lane. I learned later they had been trying to rectify some of the alterations which had been made to the play in Dublin.

I watched as several pedestrians, thinking they recognised the pair, stopped, turned their heads and stared after them. You could almost hear them muttering: "So that's the couple there's been all the talk about".

As I explained earlier, the *Yorkshire Observer* and the *Telegraph & Argus* had at that time a joint reporting staff, and that day I was working for the morning paper. "Priestley wants to talk to the *Yorkshire Observer*, so at six o'clock get across to see him at the Victoria Hotel", the night news editor instructed me.

This is my report which appeared next morning and which I include because it does give a feeling of J.B.'s state of mind.

If he hadn't been wearing a pair of dark blue corduroy trousers the serious-looking fellow with a frown might well have been a wool man pondering over the vicissitudes of a gigantic deal. He had the same blunt honesty and habit of weighing his words before he spoke as the merchants who gather on the floor of the Wool Exchange. But this was Mr. J. B. Priestley.

In a room at his hotel in Bradford last night he turned to me and said: "I believe in making it more difficult for myself!"

We were discussing the play *The White Countess* which has had its premiere at the Prince's Theatre, Bradford. Written by himself and his wife, Jacquetta Hawkes, it had not received favourable criticism at its original opening in Dublin: and yesterday's notices were not much better. But Mr. Priestley was not downhearted.

He anticipated questions before they were asked, and, now with the aid of a slapping hand and now with the help of his favourite pipe, he emphasised point after point.

Referring to a *Yorkshire Observer* critic who yesterday begged Mr. Priestley to descend "from the heights of Olympus" and to seek out again normal, ordinary characters, he explained that from his point of view the plays which had succeeded best were *Dangerous Corner*, *Time and the Conways*, *Ever Since Paradise* and *An Inspector Calls*.

None of these plays, he added emphatically, had dealt with ordinary people in an ordinary way.

"I will remind you also", he continued, "that *Dangerous Corner*, when it first appeared, had such a bad Press that the management was considering taking it off after three days".

He had the grim smile of a man about to embark on a crusade as he declared: *The White Countess* is an attempt, as all my plays have been an attempt, to do a new kind of play. It's an attempt to blend the play of ideas with a romantic background. And that's not easy, though some may say so. But I believe in making things difficult for myself.

The White Countess wasn't easy to write: it is extremely difficult to present, and it is very difficult to act. It is possible, also, that it is not too easy to understand".

Mr. Priestley halted for a moment. He was expecting Lord Vivian, who is presenting the play, to arrive, but Lord Vivian it seemed had disappeared after leaving his train in Leeds.

"We don't like people who get off at Leeds instead of coming to Bradford", remarked Mr. Priestley humorously. "Anyway, it looks as though we will have to go on without him".

Mr. Priestley said that Lord Vivian had very kindly taken the blame upon himself for the adverse criticisms in Dublin. He had been given a free hand and had altered the play to some extent.

"But I don't agree with him", said Mr. Priestley sternly. "I don't think the Dublin critics were right".

The play might have been faulty, he went on, but he thought those critics were prejudiced and they would not admit that prejudice. There were two reasons for this prejudice, he asserted. The first was that *The White Countess* was a play which took sex seriously ("And the Irish do not like to take sex seriously – they are afraid of it"): and the other because the play contained a point of view which the Catholic Church could not admit for a moment.

Mr. Priestley looked really fierce now. "A Sunday newspaper which belongs to a group which has pursued a vendetta against me for over ten years, sent a man over to Dublin to tell the story and make it as bad and as black as it could be made to look. That was breaking all the traditions of theatrical journalism.

"It is a great grief to me personally that the tactics of this sort of journalism should have succeeded to some extent in my own native town. For a day or two there was a definite hold up in advance bookings because of these tactics".

Mr. Priestley again referred to our critic, who had inferred that the playwright had used 'Time' as a theme. "I'm fed up with this nonsense", he exclaimed. "If anyone brings out a wrist watch in one of my plays they are accusing me".

He then mentioned the report in the *Yorkshire Observer* in which playgoers at the opening night gave their opinions of the play. "You will notice", he said to me, "that every woman interviewed had something to say in favour of the play.

"That is the whole point: *The White Countess* is a woman's play. And it's no good anyone saying that this is not the way a woman feels, for my wife wrote all the dialogue for Sophia".

Mr. Priestley said he still had great faith in the play which had been amended for its presentation in Bradford. He complimented the audience at the premiere and said they had been extremely attentive. "It's the easiest thing in the world to get laughs and applause", he maintained, "but it isn't easy to make an audience listen attentively to a serious work".

Then Lord Vivian arrived – a tall young man carrying a golden-tipped cigarette holder. He insisted to me that it was indeed his fault that the critics had been so severe in Ireland, and it was only because he had "booked a date" there that *The White Countess* had been presented in Dublin.

He considered the play had real merit and he was looking forward to its opening in London at the Saville Theatre.

Finally, Mr. Priestley paid tribute to the cast. Then he stood up, straightened his red tie, placed his pipe firmly in his mouth, and disappeared through the doorway – undaunted and convinced like all Bradfordians and Yorkshiremen that he was right!

On the morning this *Yorkshire Observer* article appeared, the evening *Telegraph & Argus* sent another reporter to ask Priestley if, during the interview I had had with him, he intended to imply that the Bradford newspapers had themselves used vendetta tactics before *The White Countess* opened at the Prince's Theatre.

Priestley immediately referred to a *Yorkshire Observer* headline which, two weeks before, had announced: Priestley Play a Flop in Dublin.

"What was the point of that headline?" he demanded. To the reply that it belonged to a straight news story of obvious interest to Bradford, J.B. exclaimed: "Rubbish!"

"Come off it", he went on. "That headline and story killed the advance bookings in Bradford stone dead. I am a Bradford man and I have leaned over backwards to do what I can for Bradford, as you know. That is what I get!"

Obviously upset, Priestley snapped that he could not say anything more because he had to hurry to catch a train to London. Bradford would not see him for three years.

The *Telegraph & Argus* retorted to Priestley's cry of "Rubbish!" by commenting in print: "Mr. Priestley has a reputation for being blunt and forthright. Bluntness and forthrightness when they please Mr. Priestley are all right, but when they don't please him he apparently objects to these qualities. The reports from Dublin published in the *Yorkshire Observer* and the *Telegraph & Argus* were sent by an accredited correspondent. They were fair reports and they contained no bias. The only reason our Dublin correspondent was asked to report on the play was because Mr. Priestley is a Bradfordian, and our readers are specially interested in his work, as they are in the work of all distinguished Yorkshiremen. It was a compliment therefore to Mr. Priestley that we went to the trouble to send a representative to the Dublin theatre".

It was plain from the *Telegraph & Argus* that the Bradford-Priestley "family squabble" was now out in the open; and for numerous years the relationship between the chiefs of the city's newspapers and J.B. were cool and sometimes glacial.

The White Countess was not a success in London, although I seem to remember that the excellent critic T. C. Worsley had something to say in its favour in the *New Statesman*. Its leading actor, Robert Harris, certainly found much in it to praise. "It is a play of considerable value, although it may be ahead of its time and need a few faults ironing out", he told me after the opening. "The authors have given great thought to it, and I am in full agreement with J.B. that it is a romantic comedy which should in the main appeal to women".

It is not surprising that, after the play's English premiere, Priestley should have asked to speak specifically to the *Yorkshire Observer*. This was not just because he was hurt by what he thought to be its *White Countess* shock tactics, but because he was still grateful to the paper which had given him some of his earliest writing opportunities, because he remembered it as his father's favourite morning reading, and because he knew that it continued to be held in high esteem by its West Riding buyers.

Although, owing to rising costs, its days were numbered as a daily newspaper, the *Yorkshire Observer* in the early 1950s had one of the most accomplished staffs of young journalists Bradford, or any other city, has known.

It deserves recording that under the editorship of Raynor Chapman (himself the erudite author of the extolled novel, *The Temptation of Mr Fraill*) the staff included such young men as – and I add in brackets some of their later attainments – Leonard Parkin (the much respected TV reporter and newscaster who on radio gave Britain its first news of President Kennedy's assassination), Christopher Jones (the BBC's chief Parliamentary correspondent), Jack Brooks (a great news editor of the Vancouver Sun), Michael Hill (Granada Television's news editor before joining the *Daily Mail*), Reginald Brace (probably the country's best newspaper writer on tennis), Peter Johnson (an outstanding foreign correspondent and broadcaster), Windsor Davies (broadcaster and leader writer for *The Times* and *Daily Telegraph*), Cyril Bainbridge (a valued news chief with *The Times*) and John Broxholme (after a distinguished career in magazine journalism, including John Bull, finding fame as a thriller writer under the name Duncan Kyle).

When John was younger, his family had a shop in Toller Lane, Bradford, not many yards from Saltburn Place. He served Priestley with quite a few ounces of pipe tobacco.

Another young member of that *Yorkshire Observer* staff was Alan Forrest who became literary editor of the *Sunday Reynolds News* before working for the *Daily Mail* and the *Financial Times*. From him I heard one of my favourite Priestley stories.

It concerned a TV script writer who had written a novel. The publishers said they would publish it if J.B., who was on their board and who was interested in first novels, liked it.

Alan revealed: "The fledgeling novelist met Priestley at his chambers in the Albany where J.B. stood in a dressing-gown and carpet slippers under a Renoir. 'It's all right for a first novel, lad', he said. 'Construction, excellent. Characterisation, fine, but your punctuation's terrible'. 'Ah well, Mr. Priestley', the young man said. 'I model myself on American writers like Norman Mailer. They don't worry much about punctuation. I do a first draft and then I do a second one and take all the commas and semi-colons out'. Priestley puffed at his pipe and said: 'Aye well, lad, when you get to my age, you'll start putting 'em all back in' ".

CHAPTER 16: ADMASS TAKES ROOT

I am convinced that Bradford's reaction to *The White Countess* had a more damaging effect on J. B. Priestley than has been recognised.

It must have knocked the stuffing out of his self-confidence as a dramatist as well as making him feel that his parent city had been too severe on him. From the *White Countess* onward his activities as a celebrated pioneering playwright were, with one exception, never again to blaze across the theatrical firmament. The exception was *A Severed Head* which ran and ran in London. But this was not a solo effort. He had written it with Iris Murdoch and the play was based on her novel of the same title.

Soon to follow *The White Countess*, of course, was J.B.'s comedy *The Scandalous Affair of Mr. Kettle and Mrs Moon* (J.B. called its director, Shipley-born Tony Richardson, "a clever young producer"). But although the play would have been acclaimed as exceptionally promising had it been written by a lesser writer, it lacked overall the magic Priestley touch.

Praise be that J.B. was able to pour his immense talent into other endeavours, notably what will prove to be two enduring novels, *Lost Empires* and *The Image Men*. Both are superb.

Even so, he must have had many moments of discontent. "I think of myself more as a dramatist than a novelist", he said. "On the whole I think it suits me better. I think I am a better dramatist than I am a novelist. I'm a bit of an actor myself, so it is easier to write for actors. If I'd only written the plays (and here J.B. was referring to his dazzling flood of them in the 1930s and 40s), in many respects I would have had a larger reputation than I have now because they'd be lecturing on J. B. Priestley the dramatist. As it is, they can't put me in a pigeon hole, so they leave me out altogether".

In October 1956, more than two years after *The White Countess* had been staged in Bradford, Priestley must still have been upset. For, in an article for *Yorkshire Life Illustrated*, he wrote: "I rarely visit and hardly know the Bradford of these 'fifties'. It is now filled with people who care no more about me than I do about them. If this seems a brutal statement, I am sorry; I see it as a frank declaration of the truth".

Putting it gently, the declaration didn't go down too well in Bradford. Nor did the remainder of Priestley's article.

In it he pointed out: "The Bradford of today may have in it a number of wonderful things that were not there when I was – before 1914. It may have, but I do not happen to know what these things are. On the other hand, I do happen to know a lot of good things – at least they seemed good to me – that were there in my time and are not there now".

Of the Bradford "at which only the trains of memory arrive", continued Priestley, "I not only was, but always will be a proud citizen.

"No doubt today's Bradford is really much better. No more bow-legs, rotting teeth, monstrously fat women, cadaverously unhealthy men, clogs and shawls, dirty scarves and caps, screams and curses and broken crockery late on Saturday back o' t'mill. Everybody taller, stronger, handsomer, healthier, with cars and refrigerators on the way, and the Groves, Mrs. Dale and Lady Barnett on tap. It's nearly as good now as a town in the Middle-West.

"Indeed, it has only to lose another theatre music hall, a few more enterprises concerned with books, painting and that sort of thing, to say goodbye for ever to another hundred or two genuinely original characters, to be almost exactly like a town in the Middle-West".

The article caused a local furore and intensified considerably the Bradford-Priestley squabble.

Alderman H. R. Walker, the then Lord Mayor of the city, was quick to answer Priestley. He said he was "stung by the article" and emphasised that "Surely all cities like Bradford have changed. It is bound to happen".

He insisted: "Bradford is in the forefront of the export drive because of the quality of its goods and the splendid efforts of its experienced workpeople. The reconstruction going on in the centre of the city will make Bradford one of the finest and most up-to-date cities in England. I was born in Bradford and educated at Priestley's old school, Belle Vue, and I know of no other city with better opportunities. I am proud of Bradford as I know it today, and I am proud of its citizens – despite anything Mr. Priestley has to say on the city of his birth".

The secretary of the Bradford Civic Society, Mr. H. J. Jackson, adding to the dispute, said the more he read Priestley's article, the more annoyed he became. "I think his criticisms are unsound, unnecessary and uncharitable. He has forgotten that each generation has its own standards. Modern trends are not made wrong because he does not agree with them. The evidence of his spleen is completely out of place".

It was then the turn of Alderman Dr. Kathleen Chambers, a former Lord Mayor of Bradford, to have a go. She declared: "Bradford may have changed but it has changed very considerably for the better. I think it is a better educated city. I think the people are happier than they were, and I feel that the city is developing on very fine lines".

If Mr. Priestley lived in Bradford he might change his opinion, but at the distance he was from Bradford he was hardly entitled to express an opinion, Alderman Chambers concluded.

All this over-touchiness was not something which Bradford could crow about. J.B., who since 1914 had visited his hometown so many times, had as much right as anyone, and more right than many, to give his impression of the place.

The irony is that much of what he has written was true. He didn't deny that Bradfordians were healthier, benefited from more domestic and workplace amenities, would soon have their own transport, were no longer plagued by exploitation and drunken family fights, and had home entertainment laid on by a TV screen in most living rooms.

But he did argue that Bradford, like many other English cities, was in danger of becoming indistinguishable in appearance and manners from its neighbours. Its individuality was being rapidly weakened. The Admass society had taken root.

J.B. was nobody's fool; and, culturally, Bradford at that time was in peril of becoming moribund. The Theatre Royal, where Priestley had queued starry-eyed as a youngster, had long given over its stage to a cinema screen. The Prince's where so many of his plays had been performed, would soon close and be demolished. The Empire and the Palace had vanished. And it would not be long before the Alhambra Theatre, which, in the form of variety was still trying to keep the music hall banner aloft, would have to endure hard days.

In his article, Priestley may have indicated once more that he now felt like a stranger in Bradford. Nevertheless, and no matter what he implied, the city still beckoned him. Less than eighteen months after writing the article he was back – and this time his return would make the anger about his 1956 criticisms seem almost sweet-tempered.

CHAPTER 17: THE 'LOST' CITY RUMPUS

On the morning of March 12th, 1958, I hurried back to the *Telegraph & Argus* offices to write an article for the afternoon editions. It began this way:

> I have just been playing at trains with J. B. Priestley – real ones! Backwards and forwards, to and fro went the supposed London express on a hundred yards of line at Forster Square Station, Bradford, today. And backwards and forwards with it went the celebrated Bradford author while a group of reporters and photographers grew chillier and chillier waiting for him on the icy, windswept platform. The unsuspecting newspaper men and women had, almost before they realised what was happening, been recruited to take part in the opening of Mr. Priestley's forthcoming BBC television film, *Lost City*, for which he travelled to Bradford yesterday with a screen unit. He will stay in the city for a week and will return in the spring. It is expected the film will be shown towards the end of the year.

The film *was* shown towards the end of the year – in October 1958. Yet even before it was screened it encountered many objections. They were largely directed at its title. The protestors believed it implied Bradford itself was a lost city.

Priestley, who had chosen the film's name, later explained: "The suggestion that my TV film about Bradford may have offended some people because it was called 'Lost City' is absurd. It was essentially a nostalgic piece – as the music from Brahms' third symphony must have suggested – and the LOST in the title referred to the passing of time and my youth, and I think this ought to have been clear to anybody who saw the programme".

I must be fair and point out that it *was* clear to many Bradford viewers. They realised that J.B. was searching in the film for what remained of the city of his youth – particularly those viewers who helped with the making of the programme. Priestley said that the film unit had made known to him that it was greatly impressed with the warmth of the people who assisted the making of the film. "But that does not surprise me", he commented. "That's what I expected, but I don't always get it from the *Telegraph & Argus* but I get it from the people. There is no suggestion by me that the character of the people has changed".

J.B.'s sniping at the *Telegraph & Argus* was sparked by an item which it published four months before the TV film was transmitted. It – and I hasten to say I didn't write it – read:

> "My deah, where is the Lost City?"
> "I really don't know. Sounds like a ghost town in the Wild West. Or some ancient city that was buried in the depths of South America. Or something".

"No, it says here it's Bradford".

"Bradford? Wherever is that?"

"My deah! How on earth should I know? It's LOST".

"Well, who lost it? And when?"

"I simply haven't the faintest ideah. Let's switch on and find out".

That is the sort of conversation imagined by members of the Bradford Civic Society in their nightmares.

Since they heard that the title of Mr. J. B. Priestley's television film about Bradford was *Lost City* they have been indignant. So a letter was written to the BBC Director-General.

It suggested that the choice of title was unfortunate for a programme to be televised nationally. Such a term could do harm to the city and create a bad impression, particularly in parts of Britain where Bradford was not well known.

The Civic Society put forward this alternative title: "The City I Left Behind".

If anyone thought they could persuade Priestley to change the title, they didn't know him. And if he thought he could induce his critics to change their minds, he didn't know them. All round it was a case of "No one is going to shut the mouth of a proper Bradfordian". It was a good old "family" set-to – although it did make J.B. chuckle when he said afterwards: "The film was unique among my works because it was the only one to be the subject of complaints before it even existed!"

On the day after *Lost City* was televised, the following review appeared in the *Telegraph & Argus*. It was by its TV critic writing under a pseudonym:

Pity poor Bradford! Not only has it been lost by one of its most distinguished sons, Mr. J. B. Priestley, but it remains lost.

Even the might of BBC-TV with its cameramen, technicians and producers, even the power of British Railways with its special trains, even the aid of a host of Bradfordians – all have failed to help him find it again.

Mr. Priestley's verdict on the place after a sentimental journey to put the clock back more than forty years and so rediscover the days of his youth is that while it may not be mean and shabby it is not as good as it once promised to be.

"It's not good enough for the real Bradfordian", was his last word.

Jack's judgement was pronounced as his train puffed out of Bradford at the end of a pilgrimage which he has converted into a television film entitled 'Lost City' and which, after so many delays and in the teeth of some strong criticism over the title, finally arrived on BBC-TV screens last night.

One wonders how Mr. Priestley can know what is good or bad for the "real Bradfordian". Surely the "real Bradfordian" must be one who was not only born here but who had continued to live here? Pontificating from his Isle of Wight fastness, Mr. Priestley hardly fills the latter role.

J. B. Priestley entered by Forster Square Station (an unlikely arrival point, I felt), where he met Miss Mavis Dean who accompanied him on his tour, which he undertook with the air of a sorrowing ex-Bishop surveying the crumbling ruins of his once glorious diocese.

(Miss Dean, a member of the Bradford Gilbert and Sullivan Society and a music teacher by profession, was chosen from several interviewed to fill the role of Mr. Priestley's film companion.)

From his hotel room, Mr. Priestley vainly tried to contact by telephone Mr. Mothergill (dead, alas!), Mrs. Lugden (poorly for months) and Mr. Oldenroyd (doesn't live here any more!). Did they ever exist J.B., or were they names left over from *The Good Companions*?

Then he took Miss Dean to Saltburn Place to survey the house where he spent his boyhood and to gaze on the attic where he began writing, where he made a bookcase from orange boxes.

On to Swan Arcade where he sought (but not very hopefully) for the office where he worked as a youth as "one of the worst wool clerks that ever existed" and where he learned to smoke a pipe with tobacco at threepence a'penny an ounce.

On to the markets where he had bought pennyworths of stale buns in order to save his dinner money to buy books. Then there were regretful thoughts about the Lister Park band concerts of the past and about the Theatre Royal where, in the old property room, he mused on long-lost pantomimes and Viennese operettas.

He called at the Bradford Arts Club in Mansfield Road where he chatted with Mr. Percy Monkman, went on to the Black Swan, and then looked in at the Civic Playhouse where he was president for more than twenty years.

Indefatigable in his search for the lost city, Mr. Priestley marched on – to look at St. George's Hall where he remarked on the names of Behrens, Schlesinger and Averdieck on an old programme produced by the manager, Mr. Bernard Beard.

A glimpse at young people dancing ("looks like porridge cooking") and another tear or two for the days of Chaplin and the music hall and the old Empire brought him back to Forster Square again.

Mr. Priestley did find some things about Bradford worthy of praise. They included St. George's Hall, pies and peas, the Civic Playhouse and tea-cakes.

But like Mr. John Braine (why should he be dragged into Mr. Priestley's youth?) he doesn't like the way that the "well to do" no longer live in the city. Why doesn't HE come back?

Mr. Priestley told us, by the way, that he is not a conceited man, but a vain one.

Outside the framework of J.B.'s search, I enjoyed some unusual and attractive shots of Bradford and the too-brief pictures of salesmen at work in the open market.

As a "real Bradfordian" I am unable to judge how the film entertained viewers outside this immediate area, but it's a fair bet that plenty of switching-off or switching-over was going on in places like Bournemouth, Birkenhead and Berwick!

The critic was right in one respect. There probably was switching-off in distant places, but it was mainly because – and this was not revealed – the film had been severely edited. A lot of it had ended up on the cutting-room floor.

This didn't dampen the Bradford-Priestley dispute. Numerous letters of complaint were received by the Bradford Press. Vociferous among the objectors was the director of a local concern who wrote: "During my stay of twenty-four years in the city I have seen many changes and therefore I wondered what Mr. J. B. Priestley would think of Bradford after forty years' absence from the city, but what a disappointment, what a 'flop' and what a travesty of the facts! I was appalled and disgusted at this programme being put on when everybody, I feel sure, expected to see our city as it is in 1958".

The writer of this letter had, like several other writers, completely misinterpreted Priestley's intentions when making the film.

There were opinions of another sort, though. For example, the chairman and managing director of a firm of Bradford manufacturers wrote: "Mr. Priestley was right. The Bradford we saw on TV was mostly drab – rows and rows of houses cluttered together, narrow alleys, mills, sheds and chimneys belching dark smoke. We realised that the open spaces of Victoria Square by the Alhambra or the fine architecture in Market Street are not typical of Bradford generally".

Priestley and Percy Monkman in the 'Mucky Duck', Frizinghall, during the filming of *The Lost City* in 1958. (Source: Bradford Libraries)

However, even this didn't grasp the purpose of J.B.'s *Lost City*. It was yet another instance of Bradford failing to appreciate how much, deep down, was Priestley's affection for his hometown.

"The title of the film was a good one", he reflected. "But evidently it deceived some Bradford people into thinking I was meditating an attack on my native city. It must be their consciences. Mine is clear enough on this subject".

A footnote to *Lost City*: Among the journalists on the Forster Square Station platform who found themselves, like I did, appearing in the film was Shirley Scott. Under the pen-name of Ann Riding, she had been woman correspondent with the *Yorkshire Observer*.

Not very long afterwards she married the prominent Spanish architect Carlos Sobron. They made their home in Majorca and became good friends there with the poet Robert Graves and his family.

Through Shirley and Carlos I met Graves at his house in the Majorcan mountains and the famous author of *I Claudius* and *Claudius the God* introduced me to a book he had written in the 1920s. It was *Goodbye to All That* and I quickly appreciated that it was probably the finest ever English account of what it was like to be in the trenches during the 1914–18 war.

With such a book on sale, there had been no necessity for Priestley to dwell in print on his similar wartime experiences.

CHAPTER 18: VISIONS OF WHAT SHOULD BE

It is not surprising that J. B. Priestley, who had survived, but only just, the hell of the first world war, was at the forefront of the fight to "ban the bomb and the horrors of nuclear fall-out". He believed in elevating life, not destroying it – and he rarely failed to speak out for his convictions.

In September 1959 J.B. was in his hometown once more – on the platform of St. George's Hall at a public meeting of the Bradford Campaign for Nuclear Disarmament. He headed a group of speakers who included his wife Jacquetta, the Rev. John Kemp (secretary of the Bradford Free Church Council) and F. J. Corina, a Bradford man of outstanding intellect, a Free Thinker and a brilliant public debater, who was chairman of the local campaign.

In his address, Priestley said he hoped that Bradford would say "no" to nuclear armament. Nuclear weapons, he maintained, were something that they had not asked for and had been "landed with". All they were asked to do was to pay for them and, if necessary, to die for them.

J.B. believed that Britain would not be ridiculed if she agreed to dismantle nuclear weapons, for there was more feeling against them in America and Russia than was generally imagined. From his own travels he had learned that Britain was more respected for her arts and sciences and her contributions to civilisation than for her military strength.

"The irony of it is that we have neglected all these arts and sciences to spend time, money and attention on bombs we don't intend to drop and rockets we don't intend to fire".

Then came a notable example of Priestley logic. He said: "Would it not be a brilliant and original idea to get rid of something we have no intention of using, which is costing unknown millions? Some people say we will never use them first, but we certainly will never use them second!"

The St. George's Hall meeting was followed by comments in the Bradford Press which pooh-poohed the paltry attendance of five hundred in a building which could comfortably seat two thousand. It then referred to one campaigner who, it argued, had missed the point when he maintained that Britain was already undefended because if the Russians could hit the moon they could hit any part of the earth with equal accuracy. "But", quipped the Press, "there is no risk in sending rockets to the moon, the moon can't reply".

Priestley could have retorted: "Nor could Britain reply, no matter how many nuclear weapons it had stockpiled". But this time he bit his tongue.

It was so unlike him that it was probably induced by "what's the use?" exasperation. There must have been similar exasperation a few months previously when the Bradford Press criticised him for writing *Doomsday for Dyson*, a Granada-TV play about nuclear devastation. "Mr. Priestley's object is to make our flesh creep like the fat boy in Dickens", it said. "His 'shocker' on nuclear war was designed not to make us think, but to take our emotions by storm . . . What we deplore is a line of pure propaganda which stifles argument, designed as it is primarily to scare people".

Such disdain must have disheartened J.B. And his relationship with Bradford couldn't have improved when, not long after those newspaper censures, an editorial appeared in the *Telegraph & Argus* which declared: "We are sorry for Mr. J. B. Priestley . . . He is allowing himself to grow old more quickly than he should; and in the old-man tradition he talks about the wonders of the past and the faults of the present . . . When a middle-aged man gets a bee in his bonnet it is hard to move it".

For the next five years Priestley kept away publicly from Bradford; and even in September 1964, when he became seventy, the clouds of estrangement still looked impenetrable.

Charles Leach, who at that time was editor of the *Telegraph & Argus*, recalled: "Priestley's seventieth birthday was approaching. I tried to get him on the 'phone. I thought that a man of his standing was worth an editor's special attention. But he would not come to the 'phone".

Worse, it seemed, was that J.B. announced that he had given the interview to the *Sheffield Telegraph*, and the *Telegraph & Argus* was welcome to use any material from there which it wanted.

This really was a smack in the eye for the Bradford paper. So much so that a brief announcement of J.B.'s birthday was all that was planned.

But then, suddenly, the clouds were pierced. Overnight Priestley reconsidered his attitude and the next day he told the *Telegraph & Argus* he had changed his mind. A reporter was sent to see him, and Leach told his deputy to write a leader calling J.B. Bradford's most famous son, and adding that the leader ought, also, to call for the Freedom of the City for Priestley.

Consequently, all seemed sweetness and light at last between J.B. and the Bradford Press. But it wasn't quite. There were other, if less serious, irritations between the two sides before a full reconciliation happened – even if the irritations were smoothed out temporarily by the leader article written by Ken Oddy in 1966 and mentioned on the first page of my account.

In November 1964, two months after J.B. was seventy, his long absence from Bradford was over. You couldn't have kept him away. For he was guest of honour at the open day of Belle Vue Boys' School new premises.

Described to the 400 present as "the most widely known old boy of the school", he gave a speech which quickly revealed that the rebel in him was still alive and kicking.

"Remember that a fine school must be part of a fine city, else all is lost", he urged. "I am glad to be here not just for old times' sake – it is also because I feel a school of this kind could be part of a better and finer England.

"I don't very much believe in education. Now that is a fine thing to say when you come to a beautiful new school on its first open day. Of course, in a sense I do. But for years now I have conducted arguments in private – not in public – with educationists because I argue that the real important thing is the environment".

J.B. said that however well youngsters in school were taught "if they go outside and find different and inferior values it is the different and inferior values which will win.

"So I take the view that it is folly to spend an enormous amount of money on formal education and nothing at all on the street. It is ridiculous to teach them to appreciate Shakespeare and close the theatre where you might by playing Shakespeare".

Priestley said it was impossible to over-estimate the importance of environment. "I would rather leave school at 15 and then go to work in a civilised city than be kept there until 18 and then go into a barbaric city.

"We have now here a very fine school and I am delighted to be here on this first open day, but joined with this school should be a great many things that I don't think Bradford of today – and I am not here to criticise Bradford – has".

Referring to the worry in the country about the economic position and the gap between imports and exports for which different parties offered different reasons, J.B. asked: "Is there really something wrong with us as people? Is it simply that we have a social system which isn't geared to modern industrial production?"

He wondered also whether the social system was inferior to that of other countries. "Or is it this – that the quality of ordinary life isn't good enough? That there is a certain amount of slowness, a kind of dimness, an inattentiveness, the thing that when you order something that is blue it takes over three months to deliver it and then it is red? That kind of lack of interest in what you are doing? Is this due to a lack of quality of ordinary living?"

Priestley told the gathering that as he came to the West Riding by train he looked from the window and, apart from the occasional car, he felt he might be looking at a landscape not of 1964 but 1864. Dickens, when he wrote *Hard Times*, could have seen practically the same.

"Is it simply all not good enough? We have spent a great deal of money in the last ten years but we haven't spent it very wisely".

He said he would bet anything that if anyone went back to the places he had written about in a book about thirty years ago they would not find them much better now. "Let us have, let us enjoy, and let us appreciate schools of this kind. I am proud to be here looking at it, admiring it; but let us remember that a fine school must be part of a fine city else all is lost".

Priestley's was a memorable speech; and looking back, it would be difficult to argue that it was not essentially true.

Dr. Phyllis Bentley, the Yorkshire novelist Priestley had helped make celebrated, toured the new building with him. In a recent article, she had described many of the works of her mentor as those of "a sardonic realist". Not a bad definition some may think.

CHAPTER 19: A YEAR OF PAIN AND PLEASURE

Nineteen-sixty-nine. It was a year of joy for J. B. Priestley. It was also a year of pain.

It marked the publication of his social history of the Regency, plus the second volume of *The Image Men*, his favourite novel; and his book about the Edwardians was well under way. He received a very affectionate "welcome home" from the Bradford Playhouse when he and his wife were guests for several days at its fortieth birthday celebrations. And at Bradford City Hall (as it had by then been named) the glittering silverware was brought out to honour the author with, for the first time, a full-scale civic luncheon.

The latter event was to prove ironic to say the least. For later that year, a few weeks after Priestley's seventy-fifth birthday, J.B. was denied the Freedom of Bradford. Only one among the eight responsible for making Freedom decisions voted in his favour. It was a cruel snub and it must have hurt him hard.

He showed no sign of distress to Bradford, though. But it was rumoured that in London he had said he probably wouldn't have accepted the Freedom even if it had been offered. After all, hadn't he rejected all previous top honours proposed?

If the rumour were true, J.B.'s reaction was typical of many a Bradfordian – to hide one's injured feelings behind a mask of indifference. But, believe me, he had hoped for the Freedom.

It had been a much more cheerful Priestley I met in the Victoria Hotel, Bradford, in early June 1969. With customary courtesy he had cut short a Press meeting so he could be on time for our appointment. He quickly made clear how delighted he was to be involved in the Playhouse's birthday celebrations which by then were underway. "Just like old times", he smiled joyfully.

As far as he recalled, the last time he had been in Bradford was about three years before when he came to present the first prize to the winner of a national essay competition. She was Kathleen Binns of Toller Grove. When he had read her essay about her childhood he had no idea that she came from Bradford. He was staggered when he discovered that she lived only a few hundred yards from where he used to live.

Understandably, the Bradford Playhouse chose *When We Are Married* for the centrepiece of its festivities. It was the comedy's fifth Playhouse

Percy Monkman and the Priestleys at the 40th anniversary of the Bradford Playhouse. (Source: *Telegraph & Argus*)

revival and Priestley delighted in seeing on stage again that beloved character of his, Ruby the young maidservant. She had been portrayed in the West End premiere by Patricia Hayes and by Bessie Pratt in the history-making 1938 Playhouse presentation. Bessie was to number among later triumphs her star billing in professional panto-mimes. She became one of panto king Francis Laidler's favourite principal girls, notably as Cinderella.

One evening during the anniversary celebrations, J.B. relaxed comfortably on stage in a fireside chair. In front of red velvet curtains and with a decanter of whisky at his elbow, he chatted

J.B. on the Playhouse stage when he talked informally to members. (Source: *Telegraph & Argus*)

informally for an hour and ten minutes with the audience. It included his friends Percy Monkman and Dr. Phyllis Bentley.

One observer recorded: "J.B. had the audience in stitches at his droll asides, his quick cameos, at his impromptu wit. You came to understand that it was just plain fact when he claimed he was an expert on comedians. 'They say Bradford is the graveyard of comedians', Priestley remarked. 'If it is, it isn't because Bradfordians are humourless; it's because we set high standards for our comedians'. Note the 'we'!"

During that June 1969 visit, Priestley was invited by Councillor Ted Johnson, chairman of the Bradford City Development Committee, to take a car ride with him. He wanted to show the author just how the city was improving.

"I liked what I saw", Priestley said on his return. "Whenever I'm asked if I prefer the new Bradford to the old, of course I say I don't. But it's the same with London where they've ruined the skyline with concrete egg-boxes. The problems aren't peculiar to Bradford by any means, and I admire the courage of the people who set out to change things. What I thought was excellent was the way buildings and homes are being cleaned up all over the city. And some areas are actually better than I remember them, for they have trees and grass they didn't have before. Bradford's trouble, like other cities, has been that buildings have been rushed up. I know, under pressure, buildings have to climb, but in New York, which I have been visiting for over forty years, the old skyscrapers were high but well designed".

Priestley wasn't surprised that some Bradfordians had called him "grumpy" after he had criticised some of the city's new buildings. "But I'm not really a grumbler or a grouser", he insisted. "People have just tried to hang that label round my neck. It's the oldest trick in the world for deflating criticism, however valid. You simply whisper: Oh him, he's always grumbling".

Before J.B. journeyed to Burnsall to do some painting, Jack and Jacquetta Priestley were the honoured guests, at the civic luncheon I mentioned, of the then Lord Mayor, Alderman Eddie Newby, who boasted to the diners that he had been a lifelong admirer of Priestley's works. "It would have been a tragedy if Mr. Priestley had been allowed to stay in his native city without any civic tribute being paid", he said when proposing the toast to the author.

I was at the luncheon. Just as he was leaving J.B. turned and gave me a cheeky, confidential wink. I could read his mind. "Well, it has done it. It has finally done it. Bradford has at last given me a good dinner – if nothing else", was his obvious thought. And he was right. It *was* a good dinner.

Priestley's disappointment later in the year of having the Freedom of Bradford denied him was partly offset by Bradford University's commendable decision, made in the autumn of 1969, to confer on J.B. the honorary degree of Doctor of Letters.

The *Telegraph & Argus*, to its credit, not only welcomed the news, but urged the city to go one better. It declared in an editorial: "Bradford University is to be congratulated. This honour to the city's most famous son might well have occurred three years ago when the Prime Minister was installed as Chancellor, but better late than never. The university thus joins its name to those of St. Andrew's (Scotland), Birmingham and Colorado (USA), which have already conferred on

J. B. Priestley on the occasion of being awarded an Honorary Doctorate at the University of Bradford, July 11th, 1970. Also pictured is Dr. E. G. Edwards, the University's first Vice-Chancellor.
(Source: University of Bradford)

Mr. Priestley honorary degrees. Mr. Priestley, at 75, is still in full song. He will receive his degree as a great writer of the present, not of the past. There is still time, therefore, for Bradford itself to do him the honour he so richly deserves while he remains a power in the contemporary literary scene, by making him a Freeman of the city".

On November 7th, 1970, J.B. received his honorary degree from the university's Chancellor, Mr. Harold Wilson – like Priestley, a keen pipe smoker.

In his reply, Priestley confirmed that he never changed an opinion just for the sake of novelty or controversy. His speech was almost a reiteration of the convictions he had expounded at the Belle Vue open day just six years before.

Education during the past quarter of a century, he said, had not always gone along with environmental improvements. He continued: "It is no good teaching children to read Shelley and Wordsworth if there isn't a good book shop in the city; it is no use learning to enjoy Shakespeare if there is nowhere to see the plays. The university can help to change all that".

Priestley with Prime Minister Harold Wilson, Chancellor of the University of Bradford, on the occasion of the opening of the J. B. Priestley University Library, Bradford, October 1975. (Source: University of Bradford)

Priestley and his wife, Jacquetta, on the occasion of the opening of the J. B. Priestley University Library, Bradford, October 1975. (Source: University of Bradford)

The university had already done a great deal of valuable work which helped destroy the image of the Bradfordian as a "thick-skinned, insensitive, muck-and-brass man".

"There are a few about", he said to laughter, "but Bradford has produced an extraordinary number of people connected successfully with the arts and science, and they have made a very great contribution to music and the theatre.

"With the coming of the university perhaps the whole temperature can be raised. I am a great believer in the importance of environment in connection with education".

Harold Wilson and Priestley at the opening of the J. B. Priestley University
Library, Bradford, October 1975. (Source: University of Bradford)

Before 1970 ended, Priestley who was to return to the university a few
years later to open a library and computer centre, added his voice to an
issue which at the time was saddening thousands of Bradfordians. In
other words, he gave his support to the campaign to save the city's
atmosphere-packed Kirkgate Market which he, his father and his sister
Winnie had loved when he was a boy and a young man.

He wrote to Mr. S. K. Llanwarne, Convenor of the Kirkgate Market
Action Committee, saying he would regard the destruction of this huge
Victorian building as a disaster.

"It seems to me an essential part of Bradford", he said. "And I am sure
that an enormous number of people much younger than I am share this
affection for the market and would greatly miss it. However necessary
various developments may be, it does seem to me quite wrong to sever all
links with towns and cities as they once were, and cut off young people
from all the old life of those places".

In my view, and I'm sure in that of countless others, Priestley was
speaking with wisdom. If the money it cost to erect and open the new
market had been spent on renovating the old one, then the aged but
impressive Kirkgate Market would today be a national treasure, attract-
ing visitors from all parts of the country.

CHAPTER 20: EMPTY SEATS

Although far from well, J. B. Priestley made a special effort to get to Bradford in September 1972. He wanted to see *The World of J. B. Priestley* in his hometown.

This splendid entertainment had been devised and edited by Leslie Sands from the works of the author. It was presented at the Alhambra Theatre; and in the programme Priestley had written:

> While I knew – and much appreciated – various performances by Leslie Sands in the Theatre and on TV, I didn't know him personally. It was as a stranger but a 'fan' that he first wrote to me, explaining his idea for an evening's entertainment consisting of excerpts from my plays, novels and essays. I welcomed the idea and then, shortly afterwards, the man himself. Since then, though a pair of obstinate and opinionated Bradfordians, we have got along splendidly and at this time of writing are good friends. (It is a fine thing in your later seventies to form a new friendship with such an attractive couple as Pauline and Leslie Sands). But though I have responded to some queries and made a few suggestions, so far as *The World of J. B. Priestley* is an entertainment, something for the Theatre, it is his work and not mine. On the other hand, if you dislike what you hear, blame me, not him.
>
> And two points are worth making here. If you think a Theatre evening of this kind looks all too easy, you are wrong. In fact it makes unusual demands on the director, Stephen MacDonald, and his four players, far more I would say than most ordinary plays. Finally, if it works and pleases, it will have done something rather important. It will have enlarged the scope of the Theatre, and it will have done it without undressing the cast, using shock tactics with exhibitions of violence, rape, sodomy, making the players jump down into the audience to shout at them and even manhandle them. It aims to entertain, to please without keeping to a familiar level of triviality, but making some attempt to convey some genuine thoughts and feelings about this difficult life of ours.

Priestley, together with an inflated cushion ring for comfort, arrived in Bradford on the Wednesday of his seventy-eighth birthday. The journey had taken a lot out of him and, understandably, he was irritable. His mood could not have been lightened by his memory of being cold-shouldered over the matter of the Freedom.

During the day, several television and radio interviews had been arranged for him; and a civic luncheon was squeezed between them. At this, recalled Leslie Sands, J.B. didn't behave too well, having crafty digs at the council during his address.

"After the lunch", said Leslie, "a luxury car awaited to take us to the Yorkshire Television studios in Leeds. We were behind time, but J.B.

refused to acknowledge that it was because of the length of his address. The driver, in peaked cap, slid the car into gear. We moved forward – only to stop within a few yards, at traffic lights". Leslie related what happened next:

> "What's the hold'up?" Priestley growled.
> "The lights are red, J.B.".
> "Thank God I gave up driving years ago. You ought to read that thing o' mine sometime – 'Carless at Last' ".
> "I have".
> "We might have used that in the script for the show".
> "We might, yes".
> "I know, I know". He glanced at me slyly. "Tell you this", he said, giving the poor chap another dig, "I asked for a big soft car, not a big soft driver".

What a delicious anecdote this is. It made me laugh loud because Priestley's bad-tempered retort to the driver was so typically Bradfordian. It could have been mouthed by hundreds of his fellow townsfolk had they, in similar circumstances, felt irritated, down in the dumps and short of time.

That night at the Alhambra disappointment awaited J.B. Although Leslie Sands and his actress wife Pauline Williams, together with Derrick Gilbert and Judy Loe, made Priestley's words come alive memorably on stage, there were rows and rows of empty seats – as there were on other nights of the week.

Author, playwright and actor, Leslie Sands.
(Source: *Leslie Sands*)

The big stay-away was not because J.B. had been "kicked into touch" by those who denied him the Freedom. Not many Bradford theatregoers would have been influenced by that unkindness.

No. The real reasons, I'm sure, were two. The Alhambra, badly in need of many improvements, was going through very difficult days: show after show was poorly supported. Second, Priestley by then was an old man whose works were unfamiliar to a multitude of

J. B. Priestley arrives at the Alhambra
Theatre to see *The World of
J. B. Priestley*, September 1972. With
J.B. are Charles Pick, director of
Heinemann's , who publish Priestley's
plays, and Priestley's wife, Jacquetta.
(Source: *Telegraph & Argus*)

younger people who were more drawn to writers of their own generation – if they were interested in writers at all that is.

Many of them had not only never seen any of Priestley's plays at the Bradford Civic Playhouse or the Bradford Prince's Theatre, but they would have had all on to tell you where the Prince's had stood.

With a few exceptions, classic drama and literature (and many of J.B.'s works qualify for this description) had become more and more neglected by the time of the Alhambra production – and, shamefully, were to continue being neglected.

But jewels are no less jewels when kept out of sight. One day *all* the Priestley gems will, I'm confident, sparkle in the bright light of public re-appreciation.

I hope Priestley consoled himself with such a thought after the curtain fell on the brave Alhambra effort by Leslie Sands.

Leslie was to tell me: "Priestley, who couldn't stand affectation of any sort, time-wasting and vulgarity without wit, was, and will remain, one of my favourite human beings because he was a master of words, a real Bradfordian and a genuine humanitarian".

CHAPTER 21: "GIVE HIM THE FREEDOM, BRADFORD!"

At the beginning of January 1973, four months after Priestley had visited the Alhambra Theatre, I had an appointment with the Halifax-born broadcaster and actor Wilfred Pickles. He had just appeared in a film and I wanted to talk to him about it.

However, I'd hardly got through the door before Wilfred, a great admirer of J.B., shouted out: "Have they decided to give him the Freedom yet? If they haven't it is disgraceful. Shocking! Priestley is the greatest Bradfordian alive and one of the great writers of the century – not only in Britain but the world".

All thoughts of discussing Wilfred's movie-making were forgotten. This was more important. Here, for the first time, was a public figure with "clout" saying out loud what others were whispering in private. His outcry just *had* to be reported. I made sure it was.

When I informed Wilfred there was no inkling of the Freedom being reconsidered, he exclaimed: "If the reason is political – and I've a feeling it has something to do with it – it is even more shameful".

He went on: "I love Bradford. I love its character and I love its forth-rightness. That's not smooth talk. I mean it. And because I love it, I'll give it to you straight. It is showing itself up because of Jack Priestley. He's an old man now – seventy-eight. Surely they won't deny him this honour. I'm almost certain he would be delighted with a Freedom".

Wilfred said: "Priestley's affection for Bradford is very real. His works are scattered with fond references to it. Not very long since, I related to him some of my memories of Bradford theatre of years ago. He was enraptured. He couldn't hear enough about it.

"I know a prophet isn't always hailed on his own doorstep, but really this is too much".

After Wilfred's outburst appeared in print, numerous readers wrote to local newspapers agreeing with him. I recall only one opposing view being published. None the less, it mirrored the attitude of many Brad-fordians to Priestley over the years. It came from a Shipley man who wrote: "It is a pleasing thought that Bradford and Belle Vue can help a successful writer such as J. B. Priestley on his way. But let us not forget that he left Bradford years ago and returns only to criticise the changes. If we make another Freeman of the city, why not someone who has stayed and worked for Bradford?"

Wilfred Pickles.
(Source: *Telegraph & Argus*)

Bradford Trades Council decided to do more than just join in the discussion. It carried a motion deprecating the action of the City Council in refusing to grant the Freedom to J.B. "Priestley is as much associated with Bradford as Joyce with Dublin and Lawrence with Nottingham", it pointed out.

It was characteristic of Wilfred Pickles that he should care so strongly for the reputation of Priestley. There was a sensitive and poetic spirit beneath the merrymaking and bonhomie that he brought so triumphantly to his long-running radio quiz show, "Have a Go", which had its first broadcast from Bingley and which became inseparately associated with his catchphrase, "Give him the money, Barney!" Wilfred, in fact, put together (and read over the air) what I consider to be one of the best ever poetry anthologies.

He loved fine writing and was delighted when he was engaged to read Priestley's *Bright Day* on the wireless, as everyone used to call it.

Like J.B., Wilfred was proud of his northern accent – and was once sacked because of it. He was given an opportunity as a national BBC news reader in the days when such news readers were demanded to speak with accent free voices. Wilfred managed it all right – until the end of one bulletin when he signed off: "Good night. And to my friends in the North, good-neet". That was the finish of Pickles the news announcer.

Like J.B. too, Wilfred was closely associated with amateur theatre at its best – but his first love was not the Bradford Civic Playhouse but the Halifax Thespians with whom his and Priestley's friend, Dr. Phyllis Bentley, was a leading personality.

There was another Pickles-Priestley connection. For, as a young man, Wilfred's nephew James Pickles (later to become Judge Pickles) joined Priestley's Common Wealth movement, an idealistic endeavour which didn't go the way J.B. had envisaged and from which he soon resigned.

I remember that when I was a young law courts reporter I was much impressed by the barrister skills of James Pickles; and during that period I wasn't surprised when he turned his hand to playwriting – for the good advocate and the good actor have much in common. Jimmy Pickles, as we used to call him, wrote a memorable farcical comedy for the Halifax Thespians, as well as plays for the BBC Northern Home Service. James's daughter is, of course, the actress Caroline Pickles who was superb on television as Miss Bluebell in a dramatisation about the life and career of the creator of the troupes of Bluebell Girls.

If anyone deserved gratitude for persuading Bradford to grant Priestley the Freedom of the City, it was Wilfred Pickles. His cry of "Shame!" sparked such debate that J.B. *was* finally made an Honorary Freeman of Bradford – on Saturday, September 8th, 1973.

Before the big occasion at Bradford City Hall, the *Telegraph & Argus* published another editorial about J.B. It showed how opinions can change. For it actually *invited* him to speak bluntly – an inclination for which it had criticised him more than once in the past. The paper declared:

> Yorkshiremen, of all people, should be able to forgive a man for being blunt. J. B. Priestley's bluntness has obviously delayed, for many years, the decision to bestow on him the Freedom of Bradford. However, Bradford has now decided, if somewhat belatedly, to embrace its most famous son, warts and all. He is delighted by this one honour which he obviously desired above all others. We do not know whether J.B.P. will be called to speak during or after the Freedom ceremony, but if he is he has many millions of splendid and entertaining words, which have already brought pleasure to millions, from which to choose. And we sincerely hope that he will not employ too much anxiety about choosing them. If he has some critical things to say about Bruddersford, let him say them. We want him to be blunt.

Priestley did speak at the ceremony. But not bluntly. With customary courtesy, he knew it was more a time for thank-yous. And, as his step-mother had drilled into him years before, he expressed them munificently.

As the Freedom was conferred on J.B., the Lord Mayor, Alderman Derek Smith, said: "This is an honour which, in my opinion, should have been bestowed on you a long time ago".

It was a simple ceremony in the council chamber, during which Priestley took an oath, signed the Roll of Honour as a Freeman and was presented with a scroll and casket.

Alderman Eddie Newby, the City Council's Labour leader, referred to Priestley's criticisms of Bradford. "He is not the only one to criticise the

Admission of J. B. Priestley to the Roll of Honorary Freemen of the City of
Bradford by the Lord Mayor, Alderman Derek Smith, 1973.
(Source: *Telegraph & Argus*)

new Bradford", he said. "There are members of the council on my side
who are fighting a rearguard action to save the Mechanics' Institute at
which J. B. Priestley once appeared as an entertainer. In whatever
Mr. Priestley has said he has at the same time never denied his pride in
Bradford's past".

Alderman Audrey Firth, for the Conservatives, spoke of Priestley as one
of Bradford's most gifted sons, and a man of genius. And Councillor Paul
Hockney recalled J.B.'s championing of the Godwin Street pie shop.

In reply, Priestley said: "I must thank you and thank you very warmly
indeed. You have given me a great gift and I'm proud and pleased. I owe far
more to this city than it owes to me, but at least I've told millions of people
all over the world what I know of this city, and that is a little something".

After the ceremony, Priestley, who with a wicked grin said he wanted to
make clear that "I am *not* a genius – although I do have a hell of a lot of
talent" – said he had been glad, very glad, to have been offered the
Freedom. He admitted he had fleetingly considered refusing it because
"all the fussing about it went on a bit too long". Even so he was "very
proud". And he added: "If I have criticised contemporary Bradford, it's
only in the same way I've criticised many cities in the world".

It was a happy man therefore who again walked along Market Street
where once he had lingered outside the window of his favourite shop

when it was "prodigal and glorious with tobacco itself – cut cake as thick as the other cake in grocers' shops, pressed flake a foot deep, rich harvests of Virgin Latakia, Perique . . ."

Nine days after the City Hall ceremony, J.B. was at the Bradford Playhouse which celebrated the granting of his Freedom with a production "in honour of our first president and constant inspiration".

The patrons dressed up to the nines for him; and at curtain-fall the resplendent audience remained to applaud the author out. The arm of his crumpled suit was raised in grateful acknowledgement.

The play he saw. . . ? Directed by Jean Oldfield, one of the Playhouse's most loyal and dedicated members, it was *I Have Been Here Before*. J.B. must have felt like quipping: "You're not kidding I have been here before!"

CHAPTER 22: THE HOCKNEY PORTRAIT

"We thought it would be nice if Bradford's most famous contemporary artist made a drawing of Bradford's most famous literary figure of a previous generation", said John Thompson, the city's Director of Art Gallery and Museums, when it was announced that David Hockney had accepted a commission to draw a portrait of Priestley. The picture was to complement J.B.'s Freedom and would be the first Hockney drawing to go into the Bradford collection, although the art gallery did have a collection of David's prints.

Paul Hockney, then a Bradford Liberal councillor, had urged his brother, as always a busy man, to accept the commission. There had been little need. Hockney, like Priestley, was delighted with the idea.

At the time, Priestley had completed hundreds of his own paintings, many in secrecy. And at the Freedom ceremony he gave Bradford gouache paintings of Ingleborough and Coverdale he had done when on holidays – as well as finely bound copies of *The Image Men*, *Essays of Five Decades* and a collection of his radio Postscripts.

"Painters are happier than writers", J.B. said. "As a day to day existence, painting is more rewarding than writing. I have painted abstracts, but I mainly do landscapes. I have painted Jacquetta, but I think I must have some sort of psychological block about painting people. As a playwright and novelist, I spend most of my time with people. As a painter, I like to get away from them".

Priestley, whose collection of paintings included some Sickerts and a Utrillo, was pacing up and down at his Albany, London, flat when David Hockney arrived to carry out the commission.

"About time too, my friend", J.B. said to his fellow Bradfordian, thus adding to his reputation for straight speaking. Hockney was half an hour late. It couldn't have pleased Priestley who always attempted to arrive for appointments on time.

Quickly, however, the two were chatting happily as David prepared for the drawing. With his beloved pipe in his hand, J.B. relaxed in an armchair as Hockney – "I'm afraid I draw very slowly" – began work. The outcome was a revelation. David's study of Priestley superbly captured much of the sitter's character.

Priestley's thoughts must have flashed back to the day when Epstein, the sculptor, completed a bust of him. With straight face, he jestingly commented: "Epstein, I look upon this bust as an insurance for both of

David Hockney starts portrait of J. B. Priestley. September 1973.
(Source: *Telegraph & Argus*)

us against getting forgotten. If you get forgotten there is your bust of ME, and if I get forgotten there is YOUR bust of me". If J.B. had swapped the word 'bust' for 'drawing' he could have said the same to Hockney.

Hockney's portrait was, of course, destined for Bradford. But Priestley had his own pictorial memento of his most memorable day there. With his usual flair for self-mockery, he recalled it humorously in this way: "As a souvenir of that Freedom of the City affair in Bradford, the Town Clerk kindly sent me a coloured photograph of myself, about twelve inches by fourteen inches and handsomely mounted. I am gazing benevolently out of it, holding a pipe in one hand and in the other a picture, one of my own, presented to the City Council. Everybody living in or visiting this house warmly admired this photograph, and so did I for a time. But then the oftener I glanced at it the more I began to entertain certain doubts, spiced with self-derision. And now I am sure I am looking at the portrait of a complacent old phoney – NOT ME!"

In more serious vein, Priestley knew he was old – and hated it when it came to fighting to put on his trousers and socks and to other everyday struggles. Yet he didn't lose his keenness for the wonders of life. "His enthusiasm was astonishing", said his sister Winnie.

J. B. Priestley
by David Hockney, 1973.
(Courtesy: Bradford Arts, Museums
and Libraries Service)

Among his keenness was his love of sport; and in earlier days he had been a fine tennis and table-tennis player. "I'm a cricket fan too", he said, "and I for one drop all work when Test matches are being televised".

He then made this pertinent statement: "Fred Trueman and I have one thing in common. In his own way he has had the same sort of thing to contend with as I have – stories have been made up about him.

"After the last war there grew an image of me as an old sod. I'm not. The Jolly Jack business was, I think, just a sarcastic description. I have seen myself described as a shrewd north countryman who knew how to tickle the public's fancy. This is miles out. I am not shrewd – I wish I was – and the only fancy I know how to tickle is my own".

When not glancing at the picture of "a complacent old phoney", Priestley was busy writing as usual – this time completing a book which would give me, as well as J.B., much enjoyment. Appropriately it was titled *Particular Pleasures* and it was published in the late summer of 1975, almost coinciding with J.B.'s eighty-first birthday.

A week or two after the book was published I received a hurried letter from J.B. in which he said: "I have just read and appreciated your piece on *Particular Pleasures*. There is always time to say "thank you' All good wishes".

Priestley rarely, if ever, commented on a book notice, so I was flattered. I include a section of the review here, not because J.B. liked it, but because it may indicate *why* he liked it, highlighting as it does some Priestley qualities with which he must have agreed.

Ladies and gentlemen, lads and lasses, boys and girls, please raise your glasses to the long life and happiness of the almost complete man.

J. B. Priestley was eighty-one on Saturday and although he would maintain there are rocks still lurking to buffet his serenity, perceptive observers must liken him to a stately river approaching the estuary which leads to oneness with the sea. He is working as hard as ever, but his writing, especially when compared with the slapdash churnings of some of the modern school, now has a vintage mellowness. Gone are the cocky ripples of the infant stream. Vanished are the teeming tossing rapids of the middle reaches. Their place is taken by the majestically moving, powerfully tranquil flow of Old Father Priestley.

There are occasional gruff eddies, of course; the flecks of protesting foam (would we have him different?). But they are midget disturbances unable to harry the dignified current. That current is now one of such wisdom (and not a little humour) that it is clear that this son of Bradford has wasted no moment of his long life – or failed to learn from them – or failed to pass that learning on. He is well in sight of becoming the completely fulfilled and fulfilling man. That is why I ask you, adult or youngster, to drink that toast to the man.

Some of the intellectuals may not join you. As a man of letters, Jack Priestley is too much a man of the people for their egg-headed tastes. But it is their loss, not ours. They are unaware that his un-common sense is worth more than a library of their tomes; or that the disciplined simplicity of his writing hides an understanding of life, a wonder at its marvels and a genuine grief over its hurts that they can do no more than theorise about.

Next Monday, Heinemann will publish his latest book, *Particular Pleasures*. It contains ninety-three essays about painters, composers, actors and clowns, all of whom have given him delight.

Although he says the book is a personal record in which caprice rules and in which he is indulging his whims, such modesty must not be allowed to hide the truth. For here is the work of a great and wise critic, some of the theatrical essays deserving to be put alongside appraisals by Hazlitt, Archer, Montague, Beerbohm and Agate. As for his observations on artists and musicians, their full-blooded joy makes you aware of how arid most of today's art and music criticism is.

In 1960 Mr. Priestley astounded the scholars with his knowledge of books in *Literature and Western Man*. Now he proves he is no dwarf when it comes to assessing the gifts of creators as diverse as Hogarth, Turner, Cezanne and Paul Nash; as Verdi, Elgar, Mahler and Bela Bartok; as Laurence Olivier, Alec Guiness, George C. Scott, Charles Laughton and Humphrey Bogart; as Tommy Cooper, Jack Benny, the Marx Brothers and Morecambe and Wise.

There is little room for extracts here, but the following I found typically revealing:

Of Marilyn Monroe: "She brushed aside the calendar of Playboy-style tantalizer, stepping out of the dark carapace of her actual experience, to present us with an image at once charming and convincing, of half-bewildered innocence. To have done this more than once, with almost everything against her, transforms her from 'a dish' into a remarkable serious actress. I care nothing for her wanton legend; it is her work, coming out of both hope and desperation that I praise; and I lament her wretched end and miss her".

And of Tony Hancock: "There was an inner Hancock, the one who drove him to buy large works on philosophy, which he had not the patience to master. This other Hancock, I am convinced, despised and detested showbiz. He was the dazzlingly popular comedian's implacable enemy. He was bent on ruining that career which was to be more and more impressive . . . There cannot have been many more notable and poignant example of the Tragic Clown. The final irony is that he hated pathos, and now seems nothing if not pathetic.

CHAPTER 23: THE CURTAIN FALLS

The old warrior had mellowed all right, but this doesn't mean Priestley had quelled his rebel spirit too rigorously.

In March 1974 he made a special visit to present prizes at the Bradford Royal Infirmary – and took the opportunity to let fly at junior doctors.

Before he did so, he had the large audience of nurses – if you'll forgive the expression – in stitches with his humorous stories. Many of those listening must have reminded him of the pretty Bradford girls of his youth; and doubtless he noticed more than one had "saucy curls".

J.B. confessed that hospitals were about the only things he was afraid of. "I'm not much afraid of death, but I'm terrified of hospitals because I shall be eighty in a few months and may have some terrible stroke or something. I will be taken into hospital, and young doctors who think of humans as machines instead of people may want to keep me alive as a vegetable instead of letting me die peacefully".

Nurses, overworked and underpaid, had his sympathy, he said. "But the reason why you are overworked and underpaid is because you have entered your profession from a sense of vocation, as I entered mine."

Working at something that one knew was wanted was, he maintained the supreme satisfaction at a time when fifty per cent of people did not know why or what they were doing, and whose lives seemed meaningless.

He then referred to some of the nurses he encountered in a hospital during the 1914–18 war. "They were a long way from Florence Nightingale. They were monsters. They cared nothing about pain but a great deal about counterpane. It was not your health but your neatness they were worried about".

Two years later, the first world war was again in Priestley's thoughts when he met with a fellow veteran in Bradford.

J.B. was involved in the making of a TV film based on his 1934 *English Journey*. In the book he had described vividly a Bradford reunion of Tykes who, like he, had fought with the 10th Battalion, the Duke of Wellington's Regiment.

In the book he had recorded how he encountered at the reunion a former soldier he had known as "little Paddy". J.B. recalled: "He came close to me, finished his beer and asked me stammeringly as ever, if I remembered sending him from the front line for some water for the platoon . . . 'Nay', he stammered, 'I wasn't gone more than t-ten minutes when I c-come back, where you'd been, Jack lad, there was n-nobutt a bloody big hole and I n-never set eyes on you again until tonight'."

Before filming began, the TV unit had circulated an appeal asking former 10th Battalion men to get in touch. It had only one reply. It was from Sydney Keighley, a Farsley, near Leeds, farmer, who came to talk with J.B. in front of the cameras at the Market Tavern, Bradford, where the 1930s reunion had taken place.

Priestley was delighted to meet him, but was saddened to learn that it was impossible for more old comrades to be there. "Those who weren't killed by the war have been killed by the peace", was his wry lament before he added: "I'm half dead myself, I suppose. The nation has done with us. They don't want to listen to old men any more". This was Priestley in darkest mood.

Fortunately, one Bradford occasion remained which would bring J.B. almost as much satisfaction as that of being awarded the Order of Merit

J. B. Priestley at the exhibition held in the Wool Exchange, 1975.
(Source: *Telegraph & Argus*)

by the Queen in 1977 – a very rare distinction and one made entirely for excellence: he was rightly very proud of it.

On the last day of March 1978, and three years after the Bradford Libraries and Information Service had pleased him by assembling a Priestley Exhibition at the Wool Exchange in Market Street, eighty three years old J.B. opened with gratification the most important one-man art show in Bradford's history.

It took place at Cartwright Hall in Lister Park and on view was a price-less display of sculptures, drawings and prints by Priestley's Castleford-born friend, Henry Moore. It was Moore's first major show in Britain for ten years and the finest of its kind ever mounted outside London.

"When we give, we Yorkshiremen give a lot", Priestley told the packed gallery. Moore, he said, had brought to sculpture not only a great depth but a great wonder. "I see his work in terms of something which belongs to today, but takes me back to a million yesterdays. I am proud to be a fellow Yorkshireman".

Priestley and Moore (who were accompanied by their wives) shared a knife to cut Moore's green and white iced birthday cake – four months early because Moore's actual birthday was in July. It was prepared by the Bradford City Hall catering staff and carried the greeting: "Love from Yorkshire".

In J.B.'s case, it was a particularly appropriate sentiment because many knew he was having a struggle to get about. Travel, especially, had become a heavy burden. He confessed himself an old man who preferred to "stay in one place, light a cigar after dinner, turn on TV and go to sleep".

Nevertheless, ideas still invaded and buzzed in the mind of the man who had never sought secur-ity and never hankered after power – and how he derided those who did crave or feed on power.

Not always being able to sort out and clarify those ideas, so that he

J. B. Priestley at Cartwright Hall with the sculptor Henry Moore, 1978. (Source: *Telegraph & Argus*)

could put them down on paper, must have frustrated and tormented Jack Priestley during his later days. "I am nothing if not a writer", he remarked.

It was not quite true. J.B. had never banished thoughts of death; and his instinct that there was much more to it than we shall ever know on this earth, made him courageously religious – if not exemplarily so according to the definitions and creeds of the churches, chapels and most organised faiths.

His detractors don't make me treasure less the wisdom of his little essay in which he declared: "To live with death is also to live with life. To banish all thought of death is to begin losing the flavour, zest and quality of life. Ancient peoples – like the Egyptians, with their skeleton at the feast – understood this. Shakespeare, who knew so much, understood it too, as many a familiar quotation testifies. But now far too many people are refusing to understand it. They drive the thought and prospect of death down into the unconscious, where in the dark depths, away from the light of consciousness, death swarms and proliferates in a sinister magical existence, haunting dreams and unguarded moments of the conscious mind. In it there are now too many doors that must not be opened, too many shadowy corners unvisited. There begins to be a loss of that vital energy which flavour, zest, quality of living, all demand. We hear of rich men, hoping to refrigerate themselves out of dying, who want to go on and on and on living when they may never have really lived at all. Our doctors used to strive to keep us reasonably healthy and still possessing some dignity. Beyond that, death was welcome. But some of them now, so determined not to offer death a victory, would cheerfully turn a patient into a whimpering mummy or defecating vegetable. Perhaps the Mid-Victorians, for ever attending deathbeds and visiting graveyards, overdid it. But it is worth remembering that these same people were also more energetic and much livelier than we are. So I say again that to try to banish all thought of death, as our age attempts to do, is to begin losing the flavour, zest and quality of life".

The zest-packed life of John Boynton Priestley, the great life-enhancer, the writer of magic, the pessimistic optimist, the marveller at mysteries and the Rebel Tyke, ended peacefully shortly after midnight on August 14th, 1984, at his Warwickshire home, Kissing Tree House, Alveston, near Stratford upon Avon. Although he had been seriously ill, there was no pain.

Happily, he had lived to see his play most loved by the public, *When We Are Married*, given the recognition it deserved. For the National Theatre company had recently presented this classic comedy for the first time.

Fittingly, the part of Alderman Helliwell was played by his fellow Brad-fordian, Leslie Sands, who said at the time: "I'm chuffed all round – for Mr. Priestley, for myself and for the play which really is a great comedy. I've seen it done by top professionals and by village amateurs and it has never failed to have me in tucks".

Sadly, however, J.B. didn't live long enough to learn that another of his finer plays, *An Inspector Calls*, would not only go into the repertoire of the National, but would receive such ecstatic reviews that you might have thought it written yesterday.

For the man who regarded himself a better playwright than a novelist, the London South Bank triumphs of *When We Are Married* and *An Inspector Calls* were justly merited.

The morning after Priestley's death was made known, the Bradford City Hall bell – the one which had so often and so fondly chimed in J.B.'s memory – tolled once every minute for an hour. It could be heard loud and clear in Priestley's treasured Market Street by workers scurrying to the offices and by early morning shoppers. Civic flags were lowered as a mark of respect – and would fly at half-mast until after the funeral. "This is our way of paying tribute to one of Bradford's great men", said a council spokesman.

To those in Bradford who had known J.B., sympathies went out to his family, particularly his widow. For the love story of Jack and Jacquetta Priestley had been the stuff that dreams are made of – but dreams which had blissfully come true.

CHAPTER 24: HOME AT LAST

After a cremation, J. B. Priestley's ashes rested in the old Guild Chapel, Stratford upon Avon, where a private funeral service was held, attended by family and close friends.

The chapel is near the old Stratford Grammar School where Shakespeare was a pupil, and some claim that the young William worshipped there. If true, two lofty spectres might well have embraced in the chapel. Priestley always stood in awe of Shakespeare whose works he adored. "If the day ever comes when Shakespeare is no longer acted, read and studied, quoted and loved, Western Man will be near his end", he asserted. Shakespeare would not have held back in congratulating the spirit of a marvellous fellow writer either.

In no way am I suggesting that J.B. was another Shakespeare. He would have laughed at the very notion. But Priestley contributed so many wonders to literature and the theatre that the two would have been happy and at ease in each other's company.

In October 1984 there was a moving memorial service for J.B. at Westminster Abbey. In addition to the family, those there included Priestley's friend for more than fifty years, Dame Peggy Ashcroft; the Lord Mayor of Bradford, Councillor Olive Messer; her consort, Dr. Basil Messer; and the council's Chief Executive, Mr. Gordon Moore.

The following month, on November 4th, a thanksgiving service for the life of J. B. Priestley took place at Bradford Cathedral. The pews were packed. From start to finish the predominant note was one of joy, wonder and gratitude – emotions all personified at one time or other by J.B.

The mood was set by an exhilarating medley by the Boys' Symphonic Band of Belle Vue School (Priestley's alma mater) which "swung" with melodies J.B. had known in his prime. So much so that when Spread a Little Happiness was played, the conductor's over-enthusiastic baton flew out of his hand and half-way across the congregation.

Such was the zest, that the Provost, the Very Rev. Brandon Jackson, confessed: "I felt almost like skipping down the aisle".

Even so, Priestley, never being a devotee of any denomination, did cause problems. The biggest must have confronted Canon Kenneth Cook in his sermon. For it cannot be easy to label a man who refused to be compartmentalised.

Comparing J.B. with St. Paul did seem to be overstretching it a bit (it would have had the author chuckling); yet the Priestley qualities Canon Cook did extol were made vivid and his insight was affectionate and understanding. "J.B.", he told the congregation, "was the twentieth century man of invincible trust in man's potential for glory and for a freedom of personal-ness not bound by time. We should find reason for joy and be grateful for the particular good news which he furthered – his belief in the extraordinary power of the ordinary – things like goodwill, love and good humoured relationships in the small things in life. For the great mass of mankind it is the ordinary which speaks of stability and fulfilment of hope".

Canon Cook referred to the pie made famous by Priestley in his Post-script broadcast. "Against the cataclysmic events of the war, it was a powerful symbol of the ordinariness of life".

Canon Cook said that J.B. believed life had a destiny far beyond itself and that all were responsible to each other in reaching that destiny. "We don't live alone. We are members of one body responsible to one another".

Canon Cook's sermon was enhanced by extracts from Priestley's works, delivered movingly by members of the Bradford Playhouse. One of the extracts – long renowned – was from his play, *An Inspector Calls*, and centred on the importance of mutual responsibility. It was read by Peter Stansfield and stated: "But just remember this. One Eva Smith is gone – but there are millions and millions of Eva Smiths and John Smiths still left with us, with their suffering and chance of happiness, all intertwined with our lives, with what we think and say and do. We don't live alone. We are members of one body. We are responsible for each other. And I tell you that the time will soon come when, if men will not learn that lesson, then they will be taught it in fire and blood and anguish".

What would have pleased Priestley most about the Cathedral service was that not for a moment was it a dirge of calculated sorrow. Even the lessons, read by Councillor Messer and Gordon Moore, had joy in them. For hadn't J.B. once said: "Let us not go, taking the sap and juice out of lives, in fear of death?"

Although several members of the Priestley family were at the Cathedral, Jacquetta Priestley was sorry there could not be more. J.B.'s daughter Barbara, with her husband Air Marshall Sir Peter Wykeham, was able to attend, but another daughter was ill. Priestley's son Tom, a noted film editor, was in China on an official visit at the invitation of the Chinese Ministry of Culture, through the good offices of a writer friend of the family whom his parents had unofficially adopted when he came to England during the war, Chun Chan Yeh.

Another absence, perhaps the saddest, was that of J.B.'s sister Winnie. She had fallen badly when arriving in Bradford the previous night. Even so, with arm in sling, she managed to attend the Bradford Playhouse luncheon which followed the service.

After the luncheon further readings from Priestley's works were made and Winnie was made an honorary vice-president of the Playhouse. Roger Suddards, a Playhouse trustee, said: "We have come to honour J.B. and Winnie. We do so in joy and in humility for their vision".

Jacquetta Priestley is a woman of marvellous character. For example, half an hour before the Cathedral service, she was squelching through the mud (wisely she had donned Wellington boots) to inspect the latest renovation work on the nearby, ages-old, Paper Hall in Church Bank whose preservation campaign she helped lead for some years.

Her loyalty to J.B.'s Yorkshire and particularly to his old school grew even stronger after her husband's death. It was she, for instance, who requested – a request which got the backing of the parochial church council – that J.B.'s ashes should have their final resting place in Hubberholme church yard in Langstrothdale, an area of outstanding beauty. She made the appeal, which received the approval of the Bradford Diocesan Authority, because of her husband's deep affection for the tiny ancient village and its church, within hearing distance of the calls of curlews and the songs of larks.

In April 1986 a special service was held at Hubberholme during which Jacquetta unveiled a memorial plaque to Priestley. It was inscribed: "Remember J. B. Priestley O.M. 1894–1984 Author and Dramatist whose ashes are buried nearby. He loved the Dales and found Hubberholme one of the smallest and pleasantest places in the world".

At the service Tom Priestley told how his father had relished painting the winter sky above Hubberholme, a place that he had felt was "sheer magic, not quite in this world".

When Jacquetta Priestley provided a substantial endowment for the benefit of current and future pupils at Belle Vue Boys' School, it was agreed that the school hall should be named after its most famous old boy.

The J. B. Priestley Hall was dedicated to the author on December 14th, 1989, in the presence of Jacquetta Priestley and Tom Priestley. The ceremony was attended by pupils, parents, governors and staff.

Jacquetta's kindness extended also to the University of Bradford where a J. B. Priestley Library had been established. A splendid portrait of her by artist Keith Grant was presented to the library. The picture was on loan from its owner, Nigel Weaver, a friend of her husband. Mr. Weaver agreed to the wishes of Jacquetta that it should hang in the library next to a portrait of her husband.

Tributes to Priestley were soon evident from Bradford itself. For example, the Victoria Hotel, where J.B. had frequently stayed, named one of its bars after him. And a striking silhouette of Priestley was featured in the decorative, black metalwork arch at the junction of Ivegate and Market Street.

There was another memorable tribute – but this one was made by British Rail when J.B. was 86. B.R. called one of its 100 m.p.h. locomotives after him. During the naming ceremony at Euston Station, London, Priestley shuffled over to the engine to unveil its red and silver name plate. He pointed at it with his walking stick and then, with a mischievous deadpan look, asked: "I do not have to kiss it, do I?"

To commemorate the September 1994 centenary of J.B.'s birth, seven beautiful stained glass windows depicting the life and work of the author were installed at Belle Vue Boys' School.

"When Mrs. Priestley contacted us and said she had commissioned the artist Keith Grant to produce the commemorative windows and would we like them, we jumped at the chance", said Barry Whittaker, a school governor.

Two texts were chosen, one to go each side of the windows. They were:

"To increase knowledge	"To love
to create beauty	to create
to experience love"	and to try to understand"
JBP from "Out of the People"	Jacquetta Hawkes from one of her books

"Isn't it a happy coincidence they both had written similar thoughts, at very different times? It was a marriage of true minds!", Tom Priestley observed.

Tom was right. It *was* a marriage of true minds. The convictions of Jacquetta Priestley, a rational woman of fine intellect, complemented admirably those of J.B. She cannot believe, for example, that creation is a matter of chance. There had to be "an intelligence, a transcendental significance behind the order and felicity of the Universe".

After J.B. died, it fell on his only son Tom to take charge of many Priestley affairs. "A lot of responsibility landed on his shoulders and he has been marvellous", his aunt Winnie said.

Tom, who shortly before Priestley's death acted as his father's interviewer in a splendid, biographical TV documentary about J.B., is the godson of J. M. Barrie, the author of *Peter Pan*. He was born in the house where the poet Coleridge once lived. Like his father did, Tom fell in love with the Yorkshire Dales; and in recent years has visited Bradford numerous times.

Among notable big-screen movies with which Tom Priestley has been much involved are *Morgan – A Suitable Case for Treatment* for which he won the first BAFTA Award for Film Editing, *Jubilee* and *O Lucky Man* for which he was supervising editor, *Tess* (Bradford-born actor Peter Firth starred), Orwell's *1984*, *The Great Gatsby*, *Deliverance* and *White Mischief*.

In this Central Television photograph J. B. Priestley's son Tom is seen with actor Derek Jacobi during preparation for a biographical programme Tom starred in with his father. Jacobi, now Sir Derek, used his superbly mellifluous voice to recite passages from J.B.'s writings.
(Source: Peter Holdsworth)

Tom Priestley told me: "My father was proud of his native city, proud of the beautiful countryside of the West Riding and proud of the vigorous characters he knew in his youth. If there is one feature he inherited from Bradford and passed on to me it is 'independence'; the healthy urge to lead one's life rather than try to satisfy others and live in personal misery.

"It seems that a collective Bradford would expect and demand particular behaviour from its citizens, yet could enjoy eccentricity while shaking a disapproving head. For all the direct speaking, there was an element of pomposity which he mocked in *When We Are Married* and *An Inspector Calls* – two sides of the same coin, one comic and the other tragic.

"Not only did my father accept Bradford, he relished it, and recognised it as a splendid place to be born, provincial in the best sense yet cosmopolitan, wealthy enough to provide work and generous enough to provide all forms of entertainment.

"When he left school at 16, he never then thought of 'seeking his fortune' elsewhere, but agreed to start work in a wool office. His dream was always of writing and he began young, and could see a pleasant life waiting where he would rent a cottage on the moors and write to his heart's content, earning sufficient for a simple life".

Tom went on: "The 1914–18 war changed all that, and perhaps changed him, forcing him to experience so much in the world outside. But he returned to Bradford and wrote weekly articles for the *Yorkshire Observer* while waiting to go to Cambridge on an officer's grant. He graduated in two years, then married his Bradford fiancee and quickly established himself with his first two books which attracted the attention of London literary folk. He could have followed a safe career in education, but changed it all for a life in writing, and London was where the publishers and literary periodicals were.

"My father never forgot nor abandoned Bradford and the West Riding, but he was never a Yorkshire writer, but a writer from Yorkshire, constantly returning in imagination to the Bradford of his youth, just as he kept visiting throughout the years to see his stepmother and sister and such of his friends as had survived the war.

"Working as hard as he did, and had to, he could only afford to visit them when there was a secondary reason, and this was easier when he had begun his other career in the theatre. Not only had the Bradford Civic Playhouse been born in his stepmother's kitchen, but his stepmother and sister helped to run it, and whenever he had the chance to preview a new play in Bradford he would try to find time to pop in to see his friends at the Civic.

"Tragically, his first wife and then his father had died, and he found himself with a large family to support, yet throughout the tumultuous thirties he would return to Bradford when time allowed", Tom said.

"Even in the 1939–45 war, when he was often at full stretch broadcasting, lecturing, writing novels, pamphlets, plays, occupied with all sorts of warwork as a writer, he still insisted on trying out *They Came to a City* in Bradford, and I still remember my first visit after the war for the premiere of *Summer Day's Dream*; it was still the old Bradford then in the 1940s, and I can still see the huge dark buildings and the cobbled streets.

"When the 1960s brought the rebuilding programme which tore the heart out of the old city and destroyed so much he remembered with affection, it was natural he complained, as he had always complained about anything he felt was mistaken. Perhaps this was the cause of the famous disagreement which delayed his getting the Freedom for so long; but if that had saddened him, he still delighted in revisiting the Dales and painting his gouaches there. He was always proud of the Bradford which had nurtured him, given him character and a direct way of speaking; he never studied to lose his Yorkshire accent.

"Bradford had provided the backdrop against which the dream of my father's imaginative life could be played; time and again in fiction and the theatre he drew on his memories and affection for Bradford; never more effectively than in *Bright Day*, for many people still his best novel, as it was his till he was beguiled by *The Image Man*. It might be possible to imagine Bradford without J.B.P., but not J.B.P. without Bradford".

By Tom's mentioning the many struggles his father had, the time is apt to emphasise that J.B. didn't wallow in wealth as many people imagined. And more than once he put what money he had where his mouth was.

At various times he did make a lot of money. But there were many demands on him, including his own. When, for instance his now famous first play, *Dangerous Corner*, ran for only five performances before its backers withdrew, he himself kept it running at a loss until two leading critics gave it excellent reviews and the public responded. J.B. similarly reacted when *Johnson Over Jordan*, a wonderful play, was threatened by closure after its first week.

Over the years I have heard numerous unreliable anecdotes about the riches of Priestley. One of them has kept cropping up with only minor variations. I heard it told best by Sir Peter Ustinov, who can mimic the voice of J.B. brilliantly, when we were backstage at the Bradford Alhambra.

Priestley was reputed to have been at a garden party, said Sir Peter, when a woman came up to him and asked him what he would do if he was a millionaire. "I am a millionaire", Priestley was said to have grunted sharply.

Sir Peter told me an authentic story about J.B., however, and it had me rocking. Ustinov had written his first significant book, a non-fictional one and was at a Foyle's Literary Lunch in his honour. "Priestley was in the chair and I was delirious seeing all those famous literary figures because of a book I'd written", he explained. "Suddenly Priestley said to me: 'I don't

Ian Judd's nine-foot bronze statue of J. B. Priestley erected in 1986.
(Photo: Tim Smith)

Outline of J. B. Priestley which forms
part of the wrought-iron gateway at
the bottom end of Ivegate.
(Photo: Tim Smith)

know why you bother about non-literary stuff. After all I still make a pretty penny here and there from the amateurs that are performing my plays. As for my non-theatrical stuff . . . (puff, puff) hardly keeps me in pipe 'bacco!"

The truth is that when J.B.'s will was published in December 1984 it was revealed he had left estate value at £113,570 – a sum which today would seem no more than a modest win on the football pools. It was hardly a heaped up fortune for a man whom work, work and more work had made a bright boy.

Bradford's most impressive remembrance of J. B. Priestley went on public view at noon on Friday, October 31st, 1986, when Jacquetta Priestley unveiled a nine-foot bronze statue of her late husband. Standing on a seven-foot Yorkshire stone plinth, it was a £30,000 tribute by the Council.

It was erected on a site outside the National Museum of Photography, Film and Television (on land close to where the Prince's Theatre had been) and was between the Central Library and the Alhambra Theatre.

Jacquetta Priestley, who the previous evening had been at the re-opening by Monsieur Jacques Delors of the refurbished Alhambra, was visibly delighted.

"It is a fine work of art, an incredible likeness, and full of life", she remarked of the statue created by the Leeds-based sculptor Ian Judd.

It depicted the author wearing his favourite overcoat as it flapped in the breeze. Even sister Winnie liked it. "I usually say I hate all these statues, but it's marvellous", she exclaimed.

While the statue took its first gaze at the City Hall and looked towards Market Street beyond, it was dedicated by the Bishop of Bradford, the Rt. Rev. Robert Williamson. The Lord Mayor, Councillor Bill Nunn, told the gathering, including other members of the Priestley family, that the site was particularly appropriate because of the links between "Bradford's most famous son" and the theatre and library.

Would the author have been pleased with his statue? I'm certain he would. For, in figure at least, Jack Priestley of Bradford was finally and at long last back home – for good!

INDEX

Compiled by R.J.Duckett

Note "J.B." refers to J.B.Priestley throughout.
All places are Bradford
Figures in **bold** refer to illustrations
Figures in *italics* refer to prose quoted